Jossey-Bass Teacher

Jossey-Bass Teacher provides educators with practical knowledge and tools to create a positive and lifelong impact on student learning. We offer classroom-tested and research-based teaching resources for a variety of grade levels and subject areas. Whether you are an aspiring, new, or veteran teacher, we want to help you make every teaching day your best.

From ready-to-use classroom activities to the latest teaching framework, our value-packed books provide insightful, practical, and comprehensive materials on the topics that matter most to K–12 teachers. We hope to become your trusted source for the best ideas from the most experienced and respected experts in the field.

You may also find us on Facebook, Twitter, and Pinterest.

Jossey-Bass K-12 Education

jbeducation

 jbeducation

Boosting
Executive Skills
in the Classroom

Boosting Executive Skills in the Classroom

A PRACTICAL GUIDE FOR EDUCATORS

Joyce Cooper-Kahn

Margaret Foster

JOSSEY-BASS
A Wiley Imprint
www.josseybass.com

Cover design: Michael Cook

Cover illustration: Valérie Brien/iStockphoto

Published by Jossey-Bass

A Wiley Imprint

One Montgomery Street, Suite 1200, San Francisco, CA 94104-4594

www.josseybass.com

Jossey-Bass books and products are available through most bookstores. To contact Jossey-Bass directly call our Customer Care Department within the U.S. at 800-956-7739, outside the U.S. at 317-572-3986, or fax 317-572-4002.

Wiley publishes in a variety of print and electronic formats and by print-on-demand. Some material included with standard print versions of this book may not be included in e-books or in print-on-demand. If this book refers to media such as a CD or DVD that is not included in the version you purchased, you may download this material at http://booksupport.wiley.com. For more information about Wiley products, visit www.wiley.com.

Library of Congress Cataloging-in-Publication Data

Cataloging-in-Publication data has been applied for.

ISBN 978-1-118-14109-0 (pbk.); ISBN 978-1-118-42089-8 (ebk.);
ISBN 978-1-118-42169-7 (ebk.); ISBN 978-1-118-43371-3 (ebk.)

Printed in the United States of America

FIRST EDITION

PB Printing   V10001776_061518

About the Authors

Joyce Cooper-Kahn, PhD, is a clinical child psychologist who specializes in helping children and their families manage academic, behavioral, and emotional challenges. Her approach focuses on building competencies in children, and she has particular expertise in attention disorders. A popular speaker and trainer both nationally and abroad, she is enthusiastic in her efforts to create a better understanding of how to help youth with executive function weaknesses. She is coauthor (with Laurie Dietzel) of *Late, Lost and Unprepared: A Parents' Guide to Helping Children with Executive Functioning*. She is the cofounder of Psychological Resource Associates in Severna Park, Maryland, where she maintains an active clinical practice.

Margaret Foster, MAed, is a learning specialist and leading consultant in the areas of special needs evaluations, program development, and IEP development. A former classroom teacher and frequent speaker at educational events such as the Council for Exceptional Children's conference, she has trained teachers and school administrators nationwide. She also coaches educational leaders across the globe through WIDE World, a professional development program for educators.

Acknowledgments

Joyce Cooper-Kahn: To my husband, Michael Kahn, thank you for your support, inspiration, and modeling over the years as I have pursued my various goals. You are the finest example of persistence I have ever come across.

To Lisa, thank you for introducing me so many years ago to the magnetic pull and the surprising depths and delights of relationships with children. "Stepdaughter" doesn't even come close to the way I think about you. To my son, Josh, who gave urgency to my interest in helping students with executive weaknesses, you have given back to the world, in kind, every ounce of understanding and compassion offered to you.

Thank you also to my sister, Marsha, and my brother, Gary, for your support over these last several years. To my niece, Becca, a special smile of thanks.

To Margaret Foster, my friend, my colleague, and now my coauthor. Your smarts, your sensitivity, and your commitment to doing significant work in the world are balanced by your excitement over new learning and your firm belief in a time for play. Until this book project, I had no idea that such pretty sentences could come from so rough a draft! Your friendship makes my life better.

Margaret Foster: To be an effective teacher, one must borrow ruthlessly and lend freely. In this regard, I gratefully acknowledge my fellow teachers who have shared with me throughout the years, especially Sue Stalker, Nancy Stryker, Bob Sturtz, Kathy Maidlow, Sue Gregg, Susan Jackson, Barbara Brandeen, Joy Corey, Denise O'Neal, Cheryl Schmidt, and Jane Pehlke.

Similarly, an effective teacher must be able to draw on the constant energy, challenges, and resilient humor embodied by her students. It has been my distinct honor to be a part of each one of their lives.

In a broader sense, a book like this would not be possible without the modeling of leaders in the field who work to combine theory, research, and practice. For this I am especially grateful to the people at WIDE World, who have brought these elements together so beautifully and have allowed me to be part of their work: David Perkins, Nathan Finch, Mary McFarland, Phillip Moulds, Patrick Schneiter, and Joyce Tapper-Benham.

And none of this would be of any use at all if I hadn't been involved in "practice fields" to apply my skills. For this I am grateful for the support and teamwork at Montessori International Children's House and Severn School.

Finally, I must acknowledge the good heart and true professionalism of Joyce Cooper-Kahn, friend and coauthor. She has the rare ability to selflessly reach out a hand and help those in need to find joy. I am so very grateful for the opportunity to coauthor this book with her and, more important, for her friendship.

We both thank our senior editor at Jossey-Bass, Margie McAneny, whose encouragement and expertise helped us every step of the way as we moved from idea to draft to book. Thank you also to Tracy Gallagher, senior editorial assistant, Robin Lloyd, production editor, and to the reviewers whose voices found their way into this book by supporting and questioning our early drafts. Finally, thank you to Michele Jones, whose gentle and creative suggestions included adding "a dollop" of explanatory text. We did, and the book is better for it.

Contents

For the students and teachers who walk into school buildings each day with their own hopes and dreams. May this book help you to achieve them.

–J. C-K.

To Dad, Drew, Chris, and Nicholas, and the other men in my family who enthusiastically mistake boundaries for challenges. And to all the Irish women in my life who work hard and know how to celebrate.

–M. F.

Boosting
Executive Skills
in the Classroom

Introduction

*E*very day since school started six weeks ago, you have reminded the students of the routine for starting the day. Most of the students follow the routine with ease. Except for Andrew. While the other students start their morning work, Andrew sits with all his books and folders still on his desk. Why does he need prompting to get started?

Sarah is a bright tenth-grade student who contributes to classroom discussions with enthusiasm and a fresh flow of ideas. She grasps new ideas easily, and she always gets good grades on class work. So why doesn't she turn in homework? Why are her test scores so inconsistent?

Deon races in to his middle school building on most days just as the final bell is ringing. His books askew in his arms, he generally seems disorganized and disheveled. His approach to schoolwork seems similarly haphazard. Why does he have so much trouble with organization and time management?

We used to see such students as just plain lazy or uninterested, but current studies show that there are students who are specifically impaired in their ability to organize, plan, and monitor their work.

These students have deficits in the brain-based skills that are collectively known as executive functioning. Executive weaknesses affect the ability to manage the flow of information and the tasks necessary to succeed in school.

Just as blind students have trouble negotiating their way around a room full of furniture without help, students with executive functioning (EF) problems have trouble negotiating the world of deadlines, agenda books, and paperwork. Their difficulties can range from mild to severe.

Students with weak executive functioning can be frustrating for teachers, parents, and the students themselves as they struggle to manage the "how" of school performance while they may easily manage the "what." These students need strong support and a deeper understanding from teachers to help them manage demands, demonstrate what they know, and become effective independent learners.

As an educator, you may be thinking, "How can I possibly do more than I'm already doing? How am I supposed to meet all these demands?" Our answer: work smarter, not harder!

What if the same strategies we propose for helping students with EF weaknesses also helped with the ebb and flow of your broader classroom demands?

In some ways, the process of helping students build executive skills is very much like teaching any other skill set. Drawing on sound educational strategies, we will lay out a simple and practical framework for intervention that helps you apply your teaching skills to the task of helping students with EF difficulties.

To begin, there is some specific new knowledge about the development of executive functioning that can inform your efforts. In Part One, Executive Functioning: The Basics, we offer straightforward information about executive functioning in plain language that allows you to use the information right away.

In Part Two, Interventions That Boost Executive Functions, we have compiled practical tools and strategies for working with students with EF problems. Borrowing from the Response to Intervention model, we offer interventions that vary in delivery and intensity. Chapter Three offers strategies to help you to build an EF-Smart Classroom, a classroom that is designed to support executive skills in all students, not just those with specific EF weaknesses. For the smaller percentage who need more intensive help, Chapter Four focuses on strategies that deliver extra support and instruction that can be delivered by general education teachers. In Chapter Five, we consider adjustments at the whole-school level that support both students and teachers in their efforts to boost students' executive skills. Chapter Six is for specialists and offers more intensive approaches for examining specific academic demands in light of a student's skills and level of independence. We offer a template designed to help with planning and monitoring interventions in Chapter Seven.

Our recommendations are based on a blend of research-based practices and classroom-tested experience. They are organized in a way that will help real teachers in real classrooms gain new information that can be used immediately to help negotiate the challenges you face every day.

We hope that this book will be a resource that helps you understand the needs of students with weak executive skills and the process of designing interventions for this population. With this foundation, you can pull strategies from the book as you need them and also create your own strategies that work for you and your students.

? Time to Reflect

We believe that knowledge is only a small part of understanding. Understanding also depends on applying that knowledge personally. So, at the end of each chapter we offer a few questions to consider before moving on to the next chapters.

Has someone you know been diagnosed with EF problems? If not, can you think of someone you know who has problems with organizing and prioritizing that are so significant that they regularly impact his or her life?

1. List three things that person seems to struggle with. Write down three adjectives that describe how you feel about the moments when his or her issues have an impact on you.

2. Are there some things you already know about executive functioning? Please list them so you can reference them later.

3. Do you have any "burning questions"? Write them here to be sure we've answered those for you by the end of the book.

4. If you don't know enough about executive functioning to answer these questions now, you may want to come back to them after you've read the next chapter. Remember, active engagement with the information in this book is critical to building a true understanding of the issues and their solutions.

Executive Functioning: The Basics

PART

I

There was a time when the term *executive functions* brought to mind men and women in power suits, carrying briefcases or sitting in conference rooms. Now the term has become part of the vocabulary of educators too, when they talk about students and how they manage the many tasks of school life.

Although the term has gained ground in education, exactly what it means seems a little fuzzy sometimes.

The goal of Part One is to clarify the terms and concepts associated with these critical foundation skills for learning and performance in the classroom. Grounded in the growing body of sound research, we define the terms and how they apply in an educational setting. We also review some of the factors that can affect the development of executive functions.

As you read about executive functions in Part One, you will notice that these skills have to do with more than just the details of tracking paperwork, juggling timelines, and keeping track of "stuff." (Not that those are unimportant!) It is important to remember that executive skills are the basic tools for organizing, retrieving, and coordinating the information in our own heads, all while dealing with new material and prioritizing it in light of the learning goals.

The understanding that you gain in Part One is designed to lay the groundwork for Part Two, where you will find strategies to boost executive skills in your students and ways to design new strategies for your classroom and school. You will find ideas for helping kids organize their stuff, track due dates, and monitor their workload. Perhaps even more important, you will learn about routines that facilitate students' internal organization and a more systematic approach to their own learning.

What Is Executive Functioning?

1

In the Introduction, you learned that students with weak executive functioning have trouble negotiating the world of deadlines and paperwork and that they may have difficulty juggling multiple sources of information. In order to proceed in building a working model of executive functioning in the classroom, we'd like to offer a more specific definition of the term.

DEFINITION

There are many different definitions out there, and we have tried to boil them down to their essence.

Executive functioning is an umbrella term for the mental processes that serve a *supervisory role in thinking and behavior*. It incorporates a number of neurologically based operations that work together to *direct and coordinate* our efforts to achieve a goal.

The specific operations that contribute to what is collectively known as executive functioning are referred to as *executive skills* or *executive functions*. These terms are synonymous.

It is executive functioning that allows someone to create a master plan, initiate the steps in a timely manner, react effectively to changes and challenges, and keep the goals in mind over time.

Smooth executive functioning is like riding a bike. You need to have the foundation skills in place (for example, pedaling, steering, braking, and balancing), but no single skill alone accounts for the magic that happens when you put them all together.

An experienced bike rider is fluid and sure as she navigates her path. She makes numerous adjustments to her pedaling, steering, and balance as she rides, dealing with internal challenges ("My back is getting stiff; I need to change body positions") and external challenges ("That ball is rolling right across my path!") in what appears to be an effortless manner. In addition to immediate challenges, our bike rider is considering long-term goals, perhaps monitoring the output and timing needed to meet various self-directed targets. ("I need to do a vigorous ride today to stay on my training schedule for next month's race." "I have to pick up the pace so that I can complete twenty miles and still be back home in time to shower and be ready to leave for dinner at six.")

Like bike riding, executive functioning seems misleadingly effortless in students with typical development. As most students mature and their neurological development advances, they are able to rise to the challenges caused by ever-increasing demands for independent academic functioning and long-term planning in school.

Consider for a moment, however, the students who lag behind. Although they used to get their homework in on time when the teacher required everyone to keep everything in a single bright-yellow homework folder, they may have more trouble when faced with multiple binders, rotating classes, frequent classroom and teacher changes, and daily and long-term homework to manage.

Let's return to the bike metaphor.

Second grader Jessie has always had difficulties with balance and motor coordination, but she loves to ride her bike nonetheless. When her friends started, one by one, to ask their parents to remove the training wheels from their bikes, Jessie wanted to be just like them. So, wobbly as she was, she still wanted to get those training wheels off. For weeks, she tried to get the hang of balancing without training wheels, keeping her feet just off the ground and trying to stay upright. After falling down over and over, she asked to have the training wheels put back on.

———————

Or consider an older student, John. A competent bike rider, John is racing for the first time. As he focuses on speed, he finds it harder to attend to the environment as it whizzes by. He catches a vision of something rolling across his path, but a child's ball hits his front tire before he thinks about correcting his course. He knows he needs to conserve energy for a final kick at the end of the race, but he waits too long and finds himself at the back of the pack as others speed ahead. He goes all out to catch up, but the effort tires him, and he can't maintain the pace.

———————

Like these bike riders, some kids and teens have delays or inefficient executive skills. Jessie is weak in two of the basic skills required for bike riding, so she falters when she tries to increase the complexity of the riding task. John has a different problem. He has all the foundation skills, but he runs into difficulty when he must fluidly coordinate all the components to meet the higher-level demands of racing.

We count on the fact that with time, targeted instruction, and practice, both of these cyclists will develop the skills they need. However, sometimes we have to simplify the task or offer additional support until the components come together.

CORE EXECUTIVE SKILLS

To understand executive functioning more fully, let's take a closer look at the specific skills involved.

Researchers agree on the overarching concept of executive functioning as the process of engaging in "purposeful, goal-directed, and future-oriented behavior."[1] However, there is less agreement on how to break those skills down into component processes.

Our list of core skills (see Table 1.1) draws heavily on the work of Drs. Gerard Gioia, Peter Isquith, Steven Guy, and Lauren Kenworthy and their widely used scale of executive functioning, the Behavioral Rating Inventory of Executive

Table 1.1   Core Executive Skills

Executive Skill	Definition	Impact
Planning and Organization	The ability to impose order on thoughts, tasks, play, and storage spaces	Students with poor planning and organizational skills have difficulty breaking down a task into smaller steps to reach a goal. They also have trouble creating a cognitive schema to organize information. Rather than organizing new information into a hierarchy or categories in their mind, they tend to hold on to a collection of facts. It is as if they have a file cabinet, but they just open the drawers and throw things in rather than creating files and placing information into an appropriate file folder. They may take the same haphazard approach to organizing materials as they do to organizing information in their heads.
Working Memory	Memory in the service of an action;* a dynamic process that involves reviewing new information and retrieving, holding, and manipulating stored information in our minds for the purpose of completing a cognitive task	Students with weak working memory may have difficulty holding on to multiple bits of information long enough to complete a task, such as remembering a short grocery list long enough to buy what they need or completing all the steps in multistep directions. Working memory is also critical for more complex tasks that require students to retrieve information from their own long-term storage, hold the information in mind, manipulate it in their head, and perhaps coordinate it with new input. There is evidence that visual working memory and verbal working memory are not always evenly developed in an individual.

Table 1.1   Core Executive Skills (*Continued*)

Executive Skill	Definition	Impact
Initiation	The ability to begin a task or activity and to independently generate ideas, responses, or problem-solving strategies	Without a good ability to initiate, a student may seem to procrastinate about starting tasks.
Task Monitoring	The ability to monitor one's own performance and to measure it against a standard of what is needed for any given task	Task monitoring allows someone to consider his own progress toward a goal and to adjust his plans if he is going off course. In the absence of effective task monitoring, students may not adjust the content or the pace of their work in keeping with changing conditions or feedback from the environment.
Self-Monitoring	The ability to observe one's own behavior and to determine whether it conforms to explicit behavioral expectations and unwritten social rules	Good self-monzitoring allows someone to fluidly adjust her behavior in response to overt environmental feedback and more subtle social cues, such as facial reactions or the modeling of peers. Without good self-monitoring, students will miss the signs that what they are doing is inappropriate or irritating to others, so they are prone to behavioral problems and social isolation.
Inhibition	The ability to "put on the brakes" or to stop behaviors at the appropriate time	Without good ability to inhibit behaviors and thoughts, children are impulsive and unfocused, and they tend to take action before thinking about the consequences.
Emotional Control	The ability to reflect on one's own feelings and then to use that understanding to guide one's emotional responses	Individuals with weak emotional control tend to have strong, immediate, poorly controlled emotional reactions.
Shifting	The ability to "change gears," to move freely from one situation to another, and to think flexibly in order to respond appropriately to a new or unexpected situation	People with weak ability to shift tend to get locked into behaviors or expectations, and they have trouble making transitions from one activity or pattern of thought to another.

*Barkley, R. A., "ADHD, Self-Regulation and Executive Functioning: Implications for Management and Life-Course Outcomes," presentation, Rockville, MD, September 23, 2011.

Function (BRIEF).[2] We also take into account here their later research, which identified a slightly different breakdown of skills than the original formulation.[3]

It is important to remember that these core executive skills work together to bring about smooth and efficient functioning. As an example, can you imagine a long-term project that requires planning and organization but does not require task monitoring?

Students with EF delays vary in the pattern and intensity of strengths and weaknesses in their executive profile. This book will primarily address executive skills that govern thinking, but behavioral and emotional regulation can never be fully erased from the picture, so we will offer some tips for building those skills, too.

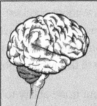

Brain Alert!

Executive skills are sometimes broken down into two broad categories: "cool" skills are those that govern *thinking* (such as planning and organization, working memory, and task monitoring); "hot" executive skills are those governing *behavior and emotion* (such as inhibiting, emotional control, and self-monitoring). The distinction between hot and cool executive functions is useful because it helps us characterize individual profiles and thus think about a person's specific needs. However, several researchers have pointed out that in real life, the hot and cool functions can never be fully separated, so the difference between hot and cool is always a matter of degree.* Barkley further explains how the neural networks involved in the two categories of executive skills work together: "The supposedly 'cool' EF brain networks, such as working memory, planning, problem-solving, and foresight, may provide for the 'what, where, and when' of goal-directed action, but it is the 'hot' EF brain network (Castellanos et al., 2006; Nigg & Casey,

2005) that provides the 'why' or basis for choosing to pursue that goal in the first place and the motivation that will be needed to get there."**

*For a review, see Hongwanishkul, D., Happaney, K. R., Lee, W.S.C., and Zelazo, P. D. "Assessment of Hot and Cool Executive Function in Young Children: Age-Related Changes and Individual Differences." *Developmental Neuropsychology,* 2005, *28*(2), 617–644.

**Barkley, R. A. *The Executive Functions: What They Are, How They Work, and Why They Evolved.* New York: Guilford Press, 2012, p. 26.

HOW DO EXECUTIVE SKILLS DEVELOP?

To understand what happens when development veers off course, it is important to know about typical development of executive skills. Our biking metaphor provides a model of how the skills unfold.

From Big Wheels to the Tour de France: The Developmental Arc of Executive Functioning

Even toddlers can get in on the riding toys! Before their small feet ever touch a pedal, they may start on a simpler riding machine. They sit on wheeled toys and push themselves along, relying on their feet as brakes when they get going too fast.

Soon these little ones progress to their first riding machines with pedals, perhaps one of those exciting Big Wheels. Hugging the ground, they learn to propel themselves with pedals. Downhill they go, learning about speed and steering as they roll. If there are busy streets nearby, it is a supervised sport. The child cannot yet be counted on to attend to obstacles or traffic or other safety concerns. Like our youngest riders, young students need help with classroom organization and routines as they develop the basic skills to support school success.

As children mature, their riding machines morph into bikes with higher seats, lower handlebars, and gears to accommodate varied riding conditions. They grow in their physical abilities and motor coordination, but they also grow in their ability to simultaneously attend to the environment. They learn to monitor what is going on around them and adjust their own actions in a fluid and consistent manner. As students, they are becoming more independent as well. They can plan assignments, monitor due dates, and manage their own homework, albeit with some prompting and supervision by parents and teachers.

In time, some of these developing cyclists may take on new challenges, such as doing tricks on ramps or racing, that add a very different level of complexity to the action. The newbie brings experience and strong skills, but these must be applied in new ways.

For example, the new racer must learn how to coordinate with team members and to train in order to peak at the right time. New levels of endurance and strength are needed, too, and each person must monitor his or her own and others' performance toward the goal of winning the race. In school, planning and goal-directed thinking are taken to a new level now. The added complexity requires better ability to hold goals in mind over longer periods of time, as well as the ability to juggle and prioritize multiple projects. Further, as the number and complexity of demands increase, so too must the student's efficiency.

Like bike riding or other arenas of development, executive skills emerge in a relatively predictable fashion as our brains mature and as we learn from experiences. Academic demands are designed to keep pace with these emergent skills.

Although a full discussion of the neurological underpinnings of executive functioning is outside the scope of this book, we offer just a bit of information in the next section to support your understanding of executive functioning when working with students.

The Brain and Executive Functioning

Although executive functioning has historically been linked most directly to the development of the prefrontal cortex (an area of the frontal lobes of the brain), it is now clear to researchers that this is an oversimplification. The frontal lobes are central in executive functioning, but these processes depend on many different brain regions that are interconnected. Problems within a specific region or in the connections between regions can lead to functional difficulties with executive skills.

Brain Alert!

As brain imaging technology advances, exciting new details on the working brain are emerging. Researchers are now able to see how the various parts of the brain operate together to complete executive tasks. Further, it is clear that different executive functions depend on different brain circuits. There is much more to learn, and fascinating new information is sure to come out of this phase of research. In a review that summarizes the state of the research, Suchy notes that "virtually all EF components require the integrity of circuits involving portions of the prefrontal cortex, the basal ganglia, the thalamus, and the cerebellum, as well as cortical areas outside of the frontal lobes . . . Suffice it to say that individual aspects of EF should *not* be viewed as easily localized."*

*Suchy, Y. "Executive Functioning: Overview, Assessment, and Research Issues for Non-Neuropsychologists." *Annals of Behavioral Medicine*, 2009, *37*(2), 106–116.

It is the natural unfolding of brain development, in combination with instruction and opportunities for practice, that leads to the behaviors we know collectively as executive functioning.

Practice and repetition set pathways in the brain, building those critical circuits responsible for executive processes. We know that these systems are late to develop, not reaching full maturity until early adulthood. The components can be seen early on, and they build on one another over time. In late adolescence and early adulthood, the thrust of development is toward greater efficiency of functioning rather than building skills.

For some students, however, delays in development of the prefrontal cortex and its support systems lead to corresponding delays in executive functioning. When this happens, the student's development will be out of sync with his or her peers and with academic demands.

✔ **To Sum Up**

- The term *executive functioning* refers to the process of supervising one's own thinking and behavior to achieve a goal.

- Effective executive functioning allows people to operate with intent, including creating a master plan, initiating the steps in a timely manner, and reacting well to changes and challenges, all while keeping the goal in mind over time.

- Good executive functioning relies on a collection of specific operations that are referred to as *executive functions* or *executive skills*. These terms are synonymous.

- There are a variety of different lists and approaches to defining the specific executive skills. We identify the following core executive skills (building on the work of Gioia, Isquith, Guy, and Kenworthy, noted earlier in the chapter): planning and organization, working memory, initiation, task monitoring, self-monitoring, inhibition, emotional control, and shifting.

- The core executive skills work together to bring about smooth and efficient functioning.

- It is the natural unfolding of brain development, in combination with instruction and opportunities for practice, that leads to good executive functioning.

- Early development is focused on building the components of executive functioning. Later development brings higher-level skills as well as better coordination between them, so students can perform more complex tasks and operate with greater efficiency.

? Time to Reflect

1. What aspects of executive functioning did you already understand well? Did you have any misunderstandings? What new understanding would you like to focus on as you move forward?

_____

_____

_____

2. Which element(s) of executive functioning are already addressed well in your classroom? Which pose the greatest problems daily for your students or for one student in particular?

_____

_____

_____

3. What changes in executive functioning do you typically see in your students over the course of a school year? How do your classroom expectations and routines change to accommodate this growth?

_____

_____

_____

4. Try to name one "burning question" you have right now that must be answered in order to solve an important EF problem in your classroom.

_____

_____

_____

5. Note any other key takeaways from this chapter.

_____

_____

_____

Putting a Face on Executive Functions: Students Who Struggle

2

In Chapter One you learned that executive functioning is a higher-order, complex set of skills that is not fully developed until adulthood. In this chapter, we offer a brief overview of students who have trouble with these skills. We also provide information about the process of evaluating executive functioning.

EXECUTIVE DYSFUNCTION: A DESCRIPTION, NOT A DIAGNOSIS

Despite widespread use of the term *executive dysfunction*, it is not a disorder in any formal diagnostic system (educational, psychological, medical, or otherwise). Instead, it describes difficulty with a cluster of skills, and may be associated with other difficulties or occur on its own.

Executive dysfunction is no more a diagnosis than is the term *fever* in medical circles. To say that a child has a fever conveys important information, but it is the associated array of characteristics that offers a fuller picture, and places the fever into a context. Is the fever from the flu? An infected finger? Hyperthermia? This additional information about the source of the problem helps us decide what to do to help. There are some general treatments for fevers, but it is the bigger picture that determines the full treatment plan.

Similarly, if we say that a student has executive dysfunction, we convey that this is an individual who has trouble with one or more of the skills that keep kids on track and moving efficiently toward goals. So this is important information and can be the lead-in to a productive discussion about the student in a school team meeting. However, it is important to remember that executive dysfunction is a description, not a diagnosis.

THE NORMAL VARIABILITY OF EXECUTIVE FUNCTIONING

Did you know that normal body temperature varies within a range based on the individual, time of day, and even what foods he or she has recently consumed? So, for example, some people tend to "run low" compared to the 98.6° standard. There is a range of normal variability.

Like body temperature, executive skills vary from one individual to another, though probably within a relatively broader range. Some people are born with the gift of strong executive potential; others are quite challenged in this arena. Most of us fall somewhere in the middle, able to manage the tasks required of us with more or less ease.

In keeping with normal variability, some of your students will require more help than others to learn to manage their time and tasks. As a teacher, you have certainly focused on building better "study habits" with many of the students who have come through your classroom. This does not mean that all those who need more help have any specific condition or diagnosis.

By tweaking the structure in your classroom, you will be able to help most of the students who fall even at the lower end of this very broad middle range that encompasses normal variability. (You will find suggestions in Chapter Three, The EF-Smart Classroom.)

However, there are some students who have more marked difficulty with one or more aspects of executive functioning. Often there is a significant associated issue that requires broader and perhaps more intensive intervention. Some of these conditions are temporary; some are lifelong issues. You will learn more about them in the following sections.

THE VULNERABILITY OF EXECUTIVE FUNCTIONING

Good executive functioning depends on many factors: sound development of several different brain regions, development of efficient connections between regions, and opportunities for learning and practice. In addition, physical health and emotional stress can affect executive functioning. Problems within any one of these arenas can lead to significant EF weaknesses. That covers a lot of territory!

Let's return again to our cycling metaphor. Let's say we are watching a bicycle race and have our eyes on an unknown novice who has lagged behind from the start. We know that she is having difficulty keeping up with the experienced racers. One observer wonders aloud if she has the speed to make the leap to the competitive circuit. Another focuses on the endurance required for a multiday race. Still another talks about the individual savvy and the team cooperation needed to pace oneself and to know when to hang with the peloton or to break away. Any one of these factors (or a combination) could lead to poor performance in the race. Understanding the possible causes will help us provide the right kind of support.

Like poor performance in a bicycle race, weak executive functioning is an outcome that occurs for many individuals with different histories and different underlying issues. Let's take a look at the most common issues that you might see in your students with executive weaknesses. This is not an exhaustive list, but will help you to be more aware of conditions affecting the executive skills of your students.

Developmental Disorders

Developmental disorder is a generic term for conditions that start in childhood and affect the course of development. Developmental disorders can cause gaps or weaknesses in a specific area, or they can affect development more globally. The most common developmental disorders that are associated with weak executive skills are attention-deficit/hyperactivity disorder (ADHD), autism spectrum disorders, and learning disabilities.

Attention-Deficit/Hyperactivity Disorder

The three hallmark characteristics of attention disorders are inattention, hyperactivity, and impulsiveness. However, these stereotypical behaviors do not necessarily occur all together in students with attention disorders. Attention disorders are not always so obvious. Some individuals with attention problems do not have the fidgety, overactive version of ADHD; instead their primary challenges may be with focusing, transitioning from one activity or mind-set to another, and sustaining attention.

Students with ADHD have an inherent weakness in their ability to manage their attention and stick with goal-directed behaviors. These students work hard just to manage the demands for directed attention on a moment-to-moment basis in the classroom, and they seem to deplete their pool of energy available for effortful attention more rapidly than other students. Students with ADHD may also be easily distracted by things going on around them or by their own internal states.

———————

For example, Liam is a bright six-year-old boy in the first grade who grasps new concepts easily and participates fully in class discussions. He is often so eager to participate that he calls out the answers during whole-class instruction. However, when working independently, his enthusiastic starts on seat work quickly give way to conversations with his peers about the latest video games or to playful roughhousing with his buddies. A youngster who has been diagnosed with the combined form of ADHD (both inattention and hyperactivity-impulsiveness), Liam has difficulty sustaining his effort and his focus long enough to complete independent tasks.

———————

Cherise is a quiet tenth-grade student who rarely speaks during class discussions and barely makes it onto the teacher's radar screen most days. She is often the last one to pick up her pen and get started on class work, but she seems to work diligently once she gets started. Her work pace is slow, so she doesn't always finish the work. Cherise gets average grades on tests and on assignments. Still, the teacher has a nagging feeling that Cherise is only half there, and in fact she is right that Cherise is often daydreaming about other things while sitting in the classroom. Cherise has been diagnosed with ADHD, inattentive type.

———————

These two students share a difficulty with attention, but that is not the only characteristic they share. It has become clear over years of research and applied interventions for ADHD that there are underlying cognitive characteristics that are keys to understanding the full impact of the disorder. Those cognitive characteristics are now understood to be executive skills. EF weaknesses are central to ADHD, and many researchers in the field define ADHD as a disorder of the development of executive functions.[1]

Now, there is considerable ongoing discussion among researchers about the best way to categorize and label the different variants of attention disorders, and you may notice that the terms continue to change over time. Regardless of how one labels a student with challenges in attention, what is most important is that you understand that ADHD represents a cluster of symptoms that includes weak executive functioning. Even when the more obvious symptoms are under control, difficulties with self-management and goal-directed behavior often derail academic performance.

Even a brief discussion of ADHD would be incomplete without addressing medications. How does medication for ADHD affect executive functioning? Medication does not improve general organizational skills, except insofar as the child is able to slow down and to utilize the strategies that have been taught. Medications for ADHD do bolster the ability to inhibit impulsive behaviors, strengthen the ability to persist on a task, and support initiation of tasks. Further, students with ADHD may be more available to learn new strategies when medication allows them to focus their attention and to be less reactive to distractions. Whether students with ADHD are on medication or not, interventions that teach executive routines and build skills for managing and coordinating learning tasks will be critical for them.

Whether or not to medicate is always an individual decision, made in conjunction with a health care professional and based on the specific needs of an individual at that point in time. There is a strong body of research which shows that medication can be helpful to a large percentage of students with attention disorders.[2] However, the real issues become lost when people either summarily dismiss the usefulness of medication or make it a one-size-fits-all recommendation.

Autism Spectrum Disorders

Another group of students in whom you may see impaired executive functions are those with autism spectrum disorders. These students, by definition, show difficulties with social communication and social interaction, and they have restricted, repetitive behaviors or interests. They also tend to be inflexible in their routines. There is great variability in the degree of severity of these difficulties; however, all students who are "on the spectrum" will show social and behavioral impairments. Individuals with autism spectrum disorders also show deficits in executive functioning. They are more likely than their peers to have difficulty with inhibiting impulses, planning and organization, and self-monitoring.[3]

Consider, for example, a sixth-grade student we have worked with.

———————

Matthew performs well in most subjects, and he becomes quite absorbed by his preferred topics. He loves history, and he has read extensively about the Civil War and military history in general. However, Matthew doesn't apply himself in some classes, and he has told teachers on more than one occasion that he doesn't "see the point in learning irrelevant information." Matthew has difficulty working in groups, because he gets stuck on wanting to do things his own way and doesn't compromise easily. He needs a great deal of support and prompting to work cooperatively with peers and to stay on top of due dates and timelines. He requires an extra measure of understanding from teachers, because his combined difficulties from both autism spectrum disorder and weak executive functions give him a stubborn, uncooperative look in the classroom.

———————

Specific Learning Disabilities

A specific learning disability is defined as an unexpected inability to learn a particular academic skill or set of skills despite having the intelligence and the instruction to do so. The origin of learning disabilities is not fully understood, although there is a presumed subtle, neurological basis.

Students with specific learning disabilities often have problems with executive functioning as well. However, accurate assessment is critical here, because EF problems can sometimes affect learning and performance in ways that look like other disabilities. Consider the following two students who struggle with reading; the first child has problems stemming from a reading disability, the second from weak executive functioning.

Emma is a fourth-grade student who was referred because she was having difficulty with even single-word reading, so she struggled to read and comprehend longer passages of text. During an assessment, the evaluator noted that Emma's errors on a word attack task showed that she had not mastered basic sound-symbol relationships, so she lacked the decoding skills needed to read grade-level material.

Stuart is having difficulty with reading in the fourth grade, too, but his has more to do with his problems with executive functioning. He does fine with decoding, but struggles with comprehension tasks. In Stuart's work with an evaluator, it became clear that he tended to read the words without monitoring his understanding, and he sometimes missed important details of the passages. When encouraged to engage with the text as he read and to ask himself meaningful questions about the content, he did just fine on the comprehension questions.

These students differ in an essential way: Emma has learning difficulties endemic to the reading process, whereas Stuart has EF weaknesses that show up when he reads. Their intervention plans will require different kinds of help.

However, they are both struggling with a routine classroom task that most of their peers can accomplish more easily. So both are likely to be depleting their energy more rapidly than their more able peers and are thus more vulnerable to poor emotional regulation, as we describe more fully in the next section.

Acute and Chronic Stress

Even though some of us have the good fortune of being strong in executive functioning, even the best among us have times when we are overloaded. Both emotional and physical stress can deplete our resources, and then we are subject to poor decision making, weak emotional control, inefficient working memory, and disorganized thinking.

There is emerging evidence that a person's ability to exert effortful attention is finite. As someone draws down her stores of available energy and continues to push herself toward a goal, she has a corresponding decrease in her ability to meet new challenges.[4]

Further, cognitive control and behavioral control both seem to draw on the same resources. So when someone is working hard to keep his attention on a task and to actively screen out the other stimuli that threaten to draw him off course, he may wind up in a state of depletion that leaves him more likely to make bad decisions or to blow up over small irritants. When a person is working hard to manage an unfavorable mood state or to control his behavior, he has little energy available for focused, effortful cognitive work.

Of course, it is no surprise to find that when people are worried about something or feeling down, their executive functioning

suffers. Or that when they are tired or hungry or otherwise struggling to regulate their physical selves, their executive functioning
suffers. Most of us shake off these routine ups and downs in our
emotional or physical states without major glitches.

But what happens when the emotional demands that our
students are facing are more intense? Acute stress from home,
school, or other major emotional concerns can dramatically
influence a student's executive functioning.[5]

When faced with a perceived threat, humans exhibit a "fight
or flight" response that prepares us for immediate action. Acute
stressors, those events that come on suddenly and that are experienced as threats to our well-being, launch us into the alarm
state and vigilant crouch of a caveman facing a woolly mam-
moth. All of our energy is directed toward protecting ourselves.
Our brains allow us to achieve this state by directing all of our
physiological and psychological resources toward basic physical survival, and in the process we cut off access to higher-order
thinking. Once the threat has passed, our arousal returns to a
more normal level, and we can think more clearly.

With this fight-or-flight model in mind, think of the many
stressful situations that students bring with them into the
classroom or that they experience even while on your watch.
When a child comes into your classroom after he has been
bullied in the hallway, for example, is he likely to be thinking
clearly? On days that a teacher comes down too harshly on
a student who is not living up to expectations, can he expect
that child to listen attentively moments later as he describes an
upcoming long-term project? It is likely that these events will
be experienced as threats, and the students will not be available for learning under these circumstances.

Does this mean that all stress is bad? Not at all. The acute
stress that we are referring to here is such that it leads to a distress-
ingly heightened state of arousal. It is clear from research that mild
stress ("I have a test on Thursday") generally activates students

and is helpful. In his classic book *The Stress of Life*, Hans Selye was one of the first researchers to point out that some stress is actually good for people and enhances performance.[6] However, when there is intense stress, executive functioning suffers.

Stress that begins early in life and lasts over time has an even more dramatic effect on students, affecting development in ways that can have lifelong downstream implications. When children are exposed to chronic stress, both the structure and the chemistry of the brain are altered.[7]

You can probably bring to mind several students whose stressful lives, each in its own way, have stuck with you in your head and heart.

———————————

Ashley is a twelve-year-old girl who lives with her elderly grandparents, who took over when their own daughter, Ashley's mother, died suddenly in a car accident. They can't afford to pay for after-school care, and they are not up to the noise and chaos of having more than one child around, so Ashley spends a lot of time alone. She worries about what will happen to her as her grandparents get older and sicker. The teacher has noticed that Ashley rarely smiles and that she seems tired and inattentive much of the time. She needs frequent repetition of directions and reminders about outstanding assignments.

———————————

Devin, in contrast, is full of energy and comes on strong from the moment he walks into the classroom. He knows everyone's name, and he calls out to kids across the room as he stuffs his books and notebooks under his chair. He has a sense of humor that is witty but just on the edge of disrespectful, and his teachers keep a watchful eye on him. When Devin has trouble with an assignment or when he gets back a paper with a lower grade than he expected, he is likely to crumple up his work and toss it on the floor, commenting angrily as he does so. Devin's parents rarely respond to notes or phone calls from school, but on one occasion Devin told his teacher that he didn't get much sleep because his parents' fighting was so loud. Most nights, he told her, he sleeps with his pillow over his head, but it doesn't always help. He says little else about his home life, and he generally responds to personal questions by saying curtly that everything is "fine."

———————

Like these two students, perhaps some of your students have experienced stretches of time when there is stress from financial pressures at home, unemployment, family chaos, or difficult family relationships. If so, you are likely to see a higher percentage of children or teens with EF difficulty.

A full review of the effects of stress on the brain is outside the scope of this book. However, there is a large body of research that links chronic stress to impaired memory and learning. A recent summary of the research noted that "exposure to highly stressful early environments is associated with deficits in the development of children's working memory, attention, and inhibitory control skills.[8]

Incorporating structure and support for executive functioning into your classroom will yield the best results for these students. (See Chapter Three, The EF-Smart Classroom.)

Depression, Anxiety, and Other Psychiatric Disorders

If you were to examine the list of symptoms that serve as diagnostic criteria for depression, anxiety, and a variety of other psychiatric disorders, you would find a great deal of overlap with executive functions.

Depression and anxiety are the psychiatric disorders that you are most likely to see, and these can have an adverse effect on executive skills.[9] You may notice slower processing, more careless errors, or less agile working memory in students whose mood has changed significantly.

What distinguishes the routine ups and downs of daily life from the diagnosable conditions we are referring to here? Whereas we all experience changes in our mood in relation to life events and daily happenings, students with significant depression or anxiety become overwhelmed by the intensity and pervasiveness of their feelings.

Jeremiah is a seventh-grade student who started the school year with the playful manner and wide grin common to confident middle schoolers. In keeping with his prior school performance, he always turned in solid work, and his test scores were mostly in the average to high-average range. Lately, though, his grades have been slipping. Jeremiah's teachers have noticed that he is less animated and seems distracted much of the time. During seat work, he often seeks the teacher's help and reassurance. "Is this what we are supposed to be doing? Is this right?" He often complains of stomachaches and head-aches, and asks to go see the nurse several times a week. The seventh-grade team leader called home to talk to Jeremiah's parents, and his mother informed him that she had noticed changes in her son's mood at home, too. A visit to the pediatrician led to a referral for a mental health evaluation, and Jeremiah was diagnosed with anxiety.

The changes in Delia's mood were of a different sort. This artistic and creative junior in high school was never a great student, but she was always involved in one school play or another. She carried a sketch pad with her wherever she went, and she often drew caricatures of her friends and teachers. Many times even the adults asked if they could keep the pictures. It was Delia's friends who first noticed the changes in her demeanor. She didn't try out for the spring play at school, saying she just wasn't interested. She hardly opened her sketch pad. Delia's teachers noticed that she seemed listless and slower in her movements and speech. Sometimes they had to tap her on the shoulder to get her attention, and one teacher noted that she seemed "sort of far away, as if there is a thin curtain between her and the rest of the class." She was late more often than usual, arriving with a brief comment that she had overslept. It was a relief to the school staff when they heard that Delia had started treatment for depression.

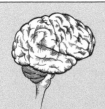

Brain Alert!

An ingenious series of studies by Tice, Bratslavsky, and Baumeister looked at the relationship between emotional distress and impulse control.* They documented that the ability to control one's behavior seems to break down under conditions of emotional distress. Rather than looking at this from a deficit model, however, they hypothesized that there might be an adaptive purpose to how humans behave in these instances. Their studies suggest that when people think that their impulsive behavior will help alleviate their distress, they are more likely to override their usual internal controls. So, for example, if you think that eating that piece of cake or skipping that class will take away your lousy mood, then you are more likely to do it. In the human organism, short-term mood regulation gets a higher priority than longer-term goals!

*Tice, D. M., Bratslavsky, E., and Baumeister, R. F. "Emotional Distress Regulation Takes Precedence over Impulse Control: If You Feel Bad, Do It!" *Journal of Personality and Social Psychology*, 2001, *80*(1), 53–67.

Students like Jeremiah and Delia show a change in their executive functioning along with notable mood changes. These changes have significant educational impact. If these students receive treatment, we can expect them to regain their sense of control and to return to their higher level of functioning. Treatment may include therapy or medication or both.

As a teacher, you can provide supports in the form of modifications, accommodations, and direct help with executive tasks, which will go a long way toward helping these students be successful while they get the other interventions they need.

Lower-Incidence Disorders Associated with Executive Dysfunction

We have reviewed some of the most common conditions associated with executive dysfunction; however, many lower-incidence disorders are associated with executive weaknesses, too. There are other developmental disorders (such as Tourette's syndrome), genetic disorders (such as velo-cardio-facial syndrome), and psychiatric disorders (such as schizophrenia) that are accompanied by difficulties with executive skills. You are less likely to have students with these disorders in your classroom, but you should be aware that ours is not an exhaustive list and that more information is available on these specific disorders.

POORLY TARGETED INSTRUCTION

With cultural shifts that emphasize competition and school-wide accountability, there is greater and greater emphasis on fast-paced curricula. However, this push comes with a cost in the form of less time for practice of the basics of how to handle learning tasks. Even students who can manage higher-level content may not be able to handle advanced curriculum demands due to the higher level of executive skills required. Some students may be able to handle one higher-level class, but falter when they must juggle many advanced classes at once.

When the executive load is poorly targeted, even able students will flounder. When both content and executive demands challenge students' abilities, more students will struggle, and they will experience undue stress.

There is a developmental timetable for executive skills just as for learning to read, and there is an upper limit to how much that timetable can be pushed. If you focus on teaching the basics of self-management, one step at a time, to a level near mastery, you will have the greatest success.

There is increasing documentation of the ability to influence executive skills at the same time that we are coming to an increased understanding of just how pervasively important these executive skills are. Teaching the basics of how to approach tasks and offering support as students mature in their executive functioning are critical classroom endeavors that should not be subject to shortcuts.

THE IMPORTANCE OF HEALTHY HABITS

Sometimes advances in research take us back to the wisdom that has endured through the ages. So it is with the connection between healthy habits and executive functioning. Recent research has underscored the ways that adequate sleep, good nutrition, and aerobic exercise can optimize brain functioning and affect executive skills.[10]

Building healthy habits will not eliminate EF problems, as there are a variety of pathways that lead to weak development of these critical skills. However, sleep deprivation, lack of exercise, and poor nutrition will exacerbate those problems and may make the difference between marginal and successful performance for a subset of our students.

Aside from reinforcing to your students the value of these tried-and-true healthy behaviors, how can you apply this research?

When students are struggling to maintain their attention and to process complex information, perhaps a lap around the gym should be a positive recommendation rather than a punitive one!

Kaplan and Berman provide strong research backing for the importance of rest breaks, or what they call attention restoration therapy (ART).[11] Restorative activities are, by definition, those that do not require directed attention and instead allow for rest of the neural systems responsible for cognitive and behavioral regulation. Rest breaks can take the form of sleep, meditation, contact with natural environments, and other activities that are minimally demanding and allow free cognitive flow without need for effortful regulation. In Chapter Three, we offer more information about ways to build pauses into the structure of your class day.

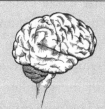

Brain Alert!

In their efforts to de-stress, many people look to television for a break. Unfortunately, television may not be as restorative as it seems. In fact, television is often a conflicted activity—there's conflict between the pull to watch the disturbing events that grab our attention in many popular shows versus the wish to look away, and conflict over the addictive pull to watch more television or not as we feel we should be doing something more productive with our time.* Further, in their review of research on directed attention, Kaplan and Berman make the distinction between activities that promote reflection and those that serve as a distraction. Television falls into the latter category.

However, it is reflection that leads to problem solving in the long run, not distraction. As Kaplan and Berman note, "In the end, this needed reflection will expedite problem solving and free directed attention resources from having to manage these persistent problems in the long run."** Unlike television, access to nature, even just looking at nature through a window, does appear to have a restorative effect on attention and memory capacity.***

*Kaplan, S., and Berman, M. G. "Directed Attention as a Common Resource for Executive Functioning and Self-Regulation." *Perspectives on Psychological Science,* 2010, *5*(1) 43–57.

**Ibid, 50.

***Please see the Kaplan and Berman article cited here for a review of studies on the restorative effects of nature.

ASSESSMENT

In this chapter, we surveyed some of the problems that can lead to weak executive skills. When a student is struggling, despite your support, how do you know what factors might be contributing? When you have lingering questions about why a student is struggling and are unsure of how to help, a comprehensive evaluation may be your best recommendation.

A good evaluation of executive functioning addresses what is going wrong and puts it into a context of the whole child. Cooper-Kahn and Dietzel summarize the multiple goals of an assessment for an individual with executive weaknesses: ruling out "look-alike" conditions, determining which executive skills are problematic, defining the severity of the problem, identifying possible co-occurring disorders, and helping build an understanding of the child's full profile, giving consideration to strengths and weaknesses.[12]

A single evaluator or a team of evaluators will assess development in a variety of areas. These tests may cover cognitive ability (IQ), language-based skills, visually based processing, visual-motor integration, memory, attention, academic achievement, social-emotional development, behavioral functioning, and overall adjustment.

By this point in the book, you have a sense of just how complex executive functioning is and how intricately linked these skills are with performance across the content areas. You can also see that different settings and tasks require different levels of directed attention, offer different levels of complexity, and require more or less ability to maintain a task focus over time. All of these will affect performance on tests. Clearly, there is no single measurement tool that can be used to diagnose executive functioning.

A review of the student's performance in real-life situations and an understanding of the history of successes and failures across settings are a critical foundation for any assessment of executive functioning. Students who perform well on tests that are administered one-on-one in an office setting may still have significant EF problems in their daily lives. For the evaluation to be thorough and comprehensive, you should expect that an evaluator will review the student's school records, ask teachers and primary caretakers to complete rating scales about the student's behavior, observe the student in the classroom (or collect information from those who observe the student), and complete interviews with the student and primary caretakers (and sometimes teachers). The expertise of the examiner is important, because inconsistency is common in students with EF deficits.

There are many tests that measure different executive skills as they present on specific tasks and in an office setting. Given the caveat that no single test can be considered an accurate indicator of executive functioning, some of them do contribute to an understanding of a particular aspect of an individual's profile. An experienced examiner will look for patterns of strengths and weaknesses that inform him or her as to the integrity of functioning, rather than focusing on single tests or subtests.

Powell and Voeller offer a succinct synopsis of the complexities involved in assessing executive functioning:

> The assessment of executive function is a particularly challenging task and has a unique set of limitations. Executive function includes a range of skills not easily measured in an office setting, where it is difficult to measure a child's ability to independently initiate and organize behaviors . . . A particularly confusing aspect of prefrontal executive dysfunction is that some adults and children can exhibit normal performance on formal neuropsychologic test measures but are highly dysfunctional in their daily lives. Thus, the absence of deficits on executive function tests does not eliminate the possibility of executive dysfunction if the

patient's day-to-day functioning is clearly impaired. Day-to-day life offers nearly limitless opportunities for distraction, disorganization, disinhibition, and dysregulation.[13]

Classroom teachers can offer the valuable perspective of someone who works with the student on learning tasks, observes the child in class, and interacts with him or her on a regular basis. Teachers' input is critical to a good evaluation.

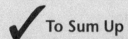

To Sum Up

- *Executive dysfunction* is a generic term that means weakness in executive functioning. It refers to individuals with a variety of different patterns, intensities, and causes of EF difficulties.

- There is a wide range of normal variability in executive functioning.

- Some of the conditions associated with weak executive functioning are temporary, and some are lifelong issues. Common conditions associated with weak executive functioning include developmental disorders, psychiatric problems, and stress.

- Poor physical health can also adversely affect executive functioning. Healthy habits such as adequate sleep, nutrition, and exercise can improve these skills.

- Goals of an assessment for an individual with executive weaknesses include defining the pattern, severity, and pervasiveness of the EF problems. It should also place the difficulties into a context of the whole child, addressing possible co-occurring conditions and describing the student's strengths and weaknesses.

- Students who perform well on tests that are administered one-on-one in an office setting may still have significant EF problems in their daily lives. For this reason, evaluation of a student's EF skills should include a review of functioning in everyday situations.

? Time to Reflect

1. Referring back to the student or group of students you hold in your thoughts (as discussed in Chapter One), is there a section of this chapter that confirms your understanding of that student? Did you discover anything new that has changed or challenged your understanding?

   _____

   _____

   _____

2. In what ways do you already manage stress in your classroom? Are there students who still show signs of stress despite your efforts? How does this stress affect their learning and performance?

   _____

   _____

   _____

3. Reviewing your EF goals and objectives for these students, do you feel that these cover their areas of need?

   _____

   _____

   _____

4. Note any other key takeaways from this chapter.

   _____

   _____

   _____

Interventions That Boost Executive Functions

In Part One we introduced executive functioning—its definitions, its multiple features and developmental aspects, and the sources and syndromes that contribute to executive skill challenges. Part Two will turn to interventions and accommodations that are designed to bring the student and the curriculum into closer alignment to create greater efficiency and success for all. Borrowing from the field of special education, we use a version of Response to Intervention to describe our approach.

The simplest way to represent this intervention model is by a pyramid. The foundation of the pyramid comprises the majority of our students. We assume that most students will benefit from good classroom structure, routines, and mind-sets. However, some students will need more targeted intervention in a small-group format. Still others—a small percentage of students, making up the top of our pyramid—will need one-on-one interventions. In Chapter Five, The EF-Smart School, we address this pyramid model more specifically. (See Figure 5.1.)

Our chapters on the EF-Smart Classroom and the EF-Smart School should address approximately 80 percent of students overall, including those with executive challenges. Our experience has led us to believe that this may be all that's needed for some students who have problems with a range of executive challenges. You will find that these chapters represent a check-list of good, solid educational practices that many of us follow often, but perhaps not all the time, or that some of us follow all the time but not within the framework and mind-set that we'll present here. In addition, because of the range of education and experience within the teaching population, it's possible that some teachers have never been exposed to these basics at all. It is a matter of applying these strategies regularly, consis-tently, and in a positive setting to make a difference for about 80 percent of our students.

Regardless of how skilled a teacher is in the full classroom setting, there are some students who cannot succeed given this structure alone. So Chapter Four, Supporting Students Who Need More Help, offers more specific strategies for working with the individual student. We find that by using more inten-sive strategies in positive small-group settings, teachers can address approximately 15 percent more of their population.

We realize that some students have more complex issues with executive functioning—often in conjunction with prob-lems of mood, attention, early academic exposure, broader learning disabilities, critical family issues, or a combination of these—that conspire to keep them from succeeding without individualized attention. In Chapter Six, How the Specialist Can Help, we address the needs of this group of students. Working one-on-one, whether short term or long term, spe-cialists can provide a more tailored approach. As students find their successes within this response level, you will slowly move them "down" the pyramid of intervention, scaffolding their support and moving them toward as much independence as they can manage. Chapter Six also looks more specifically at ways to build independence in students as their executive competence grows.

Although there is nothing sacred about the percentages cited in Figure 5.1 (you may find that your numbers shift a bit), this model helps school teams identify areas of need. These can then be addressed by rethinking schedules for teachers and specialists or by identifying physical spaces for small-group work.

Chapter Seven, Planning for Change, offers a simple yet important framework for how to assess your own unique students, classroom, and school and make simple plans for change.

Success for students depends on teams of professionals working together simply and efficiently on executive skills in ways that are unique to each school and each population. It is our hope that the following chapters will support these important efforts for you and your students.

The EF-Smart Classroom

3

Every day, your classroom is full of busy students getting ready to work, working, or trying to get out of work. They work independently and in groups. They work with students who have similar learning styles and students with opposite styles. You give lectures (short), design activities (meaningful), and assess students' understanding in a variety of ways.

So how do you manage this ever-changing cast of characters? How do you inch each one closer to his or her own greatest potential? By working smarter, not harder.

We begin our discussion of ways to help students with weak executive skills by looking at the classroom as a whole. This chapter about the EF-Smart Classroom will examine classroom design, as that provides the most broad and substantial base for all students.

By targeting how you design your classroom, you can effectively address roughly 80 percent of the EF needs in your busy classes as a whole. The other 20 percent of students may need additional strategies and plans that will be addressed in later chapters. It's important to understand that even those students who may need more specific interventions will also need the classroom strategies in this chapter to create a solid base of skills and support.

There are four broad classroom targets we'll aim at in this chapter: classroom culture, planning instruction, classroom routines, and classroom design. However, we first need to consider four "tune-up tools" or basic moves than can improve student performance: planning, repetition, time, and mind-set. We'll consider these approaches briefly and then take aim at the target elements. We hope you won't find these explanations to be too simplistic, but we want to create a common understanding of the terms so that we can use them fluidly later on.

It is important to remember that no single target or tool in the EF-Smart Classroom is meant to produce dramatic results; instead, they work together in a balanced blend that will wrap support around your students and allow them to succeed. With practice, repetition, and time, the EF scaffold that you're constructing around your students can slowly be deconstructed, and each student can move forward toward independence at the pace that's right for him or her.

THE TUNE-UP TOOLS: PLANNING, TIME, REPETITION, AND MIND-SET

As educators, we crave "small moves" than can effectively impact our students. These tune-up tools do that by examining practices and mind-sets that can make a large difference in students' learning and performance.

Planning to Plan

Many of us intend to plan carefully and to reassess our teaching strategies, but with busy schedules, we often fall into weak habits and let our planning slide. We often neglect to reassess carefully when things aren't going well. Perhaps we blame the child or the family or the fact that it's January.

Although we sometimes forget to do it, mindful planning allows us to identify a problem of practice by pausing to clarify the issues of an individual or particular group of learners, research what we and others know about the area of concern, and plan carefully for change.

As mentioned earlier, we will help you make these plans by working smarter not harder, but planning is essential.

Allotting Time

Time is probably *the* most limited commodity we have in our schools. There is so little of it, yet so much material to cover before standardized tests are given in the spring or before our students go on to the middle school, high school, or college. Despite time's scarcity, our ability to manage time well and to devote enough of it to modeling and *practicing* important executive skills is what will determine whether our students actually reach mastery. Just as though they were riding a bike too infrequently, if our students don't reach mastery, they may continue to feel incompetent and bruised over and over again. In addition to reading, writing, and math, the ability to execute a plan effectively and efficiently is one of the most important skills we can give our students. And it's our job to find and allot time for that practice!

In one school, teachers noticed that some students took a while to ramp up at the beginning of each new quarter, as if they were tired or maybe a bit too relaxed. Although the learning specialist was already providing help to many of these middle and high school students at the end of the quarter so that they could finish strong, the teachers decided that a stronger *start* was needed too! So they instituted a new plan for each student who received support services through the school's learning center. During the first week of the new quarter, the learning specialist did a daily "planner check." The learning specialist also asked the students about their work for the new quarter: "Let's see how your planner looks. Are you missing anything? Is there anything due next week?" And finally, "Have your teachers posted any grades for the new quarter yet?" This last question is usually greeted with a surprised look, which means it was a great question!

This practice took about two minutes per student, ten minutes total time for a small group, but it refocused students' attention on the organizational decisions and skills they needed to succeed.

So often it may be only a small amount of time that is needed. It may be as little as two minutes devoted to a conversation designed to help the student self-reflect. Or it may be three to five minutes at the end of each class to allow for writing down assignments, putting papers away in the right place, asking questions, and . . . breathing.

Repetition

Milton Dehn addresses the very important executive function known as working memory in his book *Working Memory and Academic Learning*. He reminds us that "the probability of long-term storage is . . . a function of how many times an item enters working memory. Thus, repeated practice and review is an effective instructional method for all students."[1] Repetition is important for building executive functioning for two reasons:

1. While repeated practice is building long-term memory, it also builds automaticity for both simple skills and complex routines. For example, when students practice simple multiplication facts using a chart, they internalize the number patterns along with the facts in a variety of ways with each exposure. This produces a stronger understanding and a script that can be easily retrieved as one chunk of information during a test. Similarly, using the scientific method as an outline for multiple lab reports creates a script or template that reduces the cognitive complexity of the assignment. This kind of automaticity reduces the load on directed attention and increases the efficiency of the executive functions.

2. Repetition ensures that students carry out complex assignments with some opportunities for failure and additional opportunities to reflect on those failures and try again for success.

It is our belief that students don't really mind repetition and even *some* failure as long as they can track their successes and have some reason to believe they can succeed in the end. Consider how often students fail on each level of a video game—they persist because they know that with repetition (and "cheats"), they can succeed.

Similarly, in the EF-Smart Classroom we need to build both repetition and tailored guidance into our classroom routines. This includes repeating a complex assignment more than once during the year to allow students the opportunity to stumble and then self-correct with guidance.

Mind-Set

"Mindsets are assumptions, beliefs, and expectations we possess about ourselves and others. They direct our behavior and interactions. Mindsets are powerful and difficult to disguise or hide."[2]

All the planning, repetition, and time in the world will not lay the groundwork for success if teachers do not lead with the right mind-set. Teachers need to cultivate a positive, supportive attitude in themselves and in their students—beginning with themselves. They need to accept the fact that their students will make EF mistakes repeatedly; they must smile at their missteps and sit shoulder to shoulder with students when they need to make repairs, whether those repairs are academic or social. Just think about when you were first starting out teaching: you wanted your missteps addressed with patience and clear guidance.

Unless you adopt this mind-set, students' frustration, anxiety, or tension will render them incapable of processing the good lessons and activities you bring to them each day. (See the discussion in Chapter Two about acute and chronic stress.) When your mind-set is negative, you respond to students in a way that can compound their frustration and anxiety as they perceive the pressure to perform but are unable to do so. Even anticipating the harsh teacher's demands can trigger the fight-or-flight response in students, redirecting their attention and energy away from the higher-level thinking processes.

In fact, a student's own history of struggle and failure can make the mildest suggestions seem harsh. Consider Bernard.

Bernard is a student who lacks confidence because he struggles with organization and planning. In his written and oral work, he often has great ideas but lacks a logical structure and organized flow. With support and the occasional opportunity to follow up with a "do-over," Bernard is learning to incorporate more structure into his work. This effort, however, was temporarily derailed during his seventh-grade year. Bernard began to make frequent visits to the school nurse, complaining of stomachaches and headaches. After several calls from the nurse's office, Bernard's mother recognized a pattern. The visits to the nurse seemed to dramatically increase in the days before Bernard's oral presentations. After a little detective work, the reason became clear—the teacher's oral feedback in front of the whole class felt harsh to him. It focused on what was wrong with his organization without offering specific praise for what he had done correctly. This lopsided feedback interfered with his progress and added an incapacitating layer of anxiety.

Remember, our students may be smart enough to recognize that they are performing poorly; they just may not be skilled enough to change without our help.

Further, it has been shown that merely refraining from subjecting students to ridicule, judgment, or harsh words is not enough to support student learning. Targeted words and interventions that convey appreciation, acceptance, and support after failure are required. These won't come easily or automatically, as you may share your students' disappointment after failed attempts, so you need to actively pursue and cultivate a positive and supportive mind-set in yourself in order to create and sustain a positive culture in the EF-Smart Classroom.

It Takes All Four

If we think of these four tune-up tools as the legs of a chair, consider what happens if any one of them is broken. A classroom with good planning, plenty of repetition, and dedicated time could be consistently harsh without the right *mind-set*.

Without *planning*, the classroom that employs repetition, allocates time, and embraces the right mind-set might work some of the time, but could feel haphazard and disjointed, leaving students without the consistent footholds they need to succeed.

Similarly, without the right amount of *time* devoted to repetition and mastery, students may feel that their successes are based more on luck than on skill—and indeed they are, as students are left working with only emerging skills, like chairs with loose legs.

Although all students will function better with these elements in place, students with weak executive functioning may fail without them. Because their "executive balance" is off to begin with, all four legs of the chair must be firmly intact!

Now that we have tuned up these basic elements, let's take a closer look at some broader classroom elements that are necessary to insure success for all.

THE TARGETS: CULTURE, PLANNING, ROUTINES, AND CLASSROOM DESIGN

In this section, we will consider four targets that will focus and center our EF work: classroom culture, planning instruction, classroom routines, and classroom design. We begin with classroom culture, as it defines everything we do, and it can either contribute to or detract from the effectiveness of all our EF work.

Classroom Culture

Classroom culture may sound like a soft, intangible element; however, it is as palpable as a strong wind and as important to learning and performance as keeping the lights on when reading. You can either cultivate an atmosphere that is accepting of a range of learning styles, or you will leave some students in the dark. Your classroom can be focused and dedicated to success for all, or windblown with success for some. Your four walls can envelope a space where each student feels comfortable or even excited to learn, or the cognitive doors to learning will remain closed.

As it would be if we were coaching a racing cyclist, our EF coaching needs to be positive, well informed, and

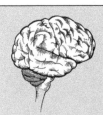

Brain Alert!

Dr. Judy Willis, neurologist and educator, talks about three brain systems that exert a strong influence on our neurological availability to learn.* She calls these three systems RAD, an acronym for the brain structures and the neurotransmitters that act together in response to stress. RAD includes the reticular activating system and the amygdala, two active systems in the brain that serve as gatekeepers to determine what information is important enough to admit into perception; and dopamine, a neurotransmitter that responds to pleasurable events by enhancing transmission of information in the brain. These systems each have a role in how we process information. When the student experiences emotionally loaded events, or when the information is just uninteresting, the new information may not advance to parts of the brain responsible for higher-order thinking. The information is virtually lost.

If you truly embrace the right mind-set and teach executive skills in a positive, meaningful, and dynamic manner, even mistakes and missteps can be tolerated by the EF-sensitive student. If you do not, even moments of instructional brilliance may not be enough.

*Willis, J. *How Your Child Learns Best: Brain-Friendly Strategies You Can Use to Ignite Your Child's Learning and Increase School Success.* Naperville, IL: Sourcebooks, 2008.

relentless. Indeed, what coach would greet their athlete at the beginning of a training session or race with "Not you again!" We make it a practice to smile and say the student's name when we see him or her walk through the door. With this same mind-set, the EF-Smart Classroom is designed, inside and out, to support success for all, and it has a classroom culture that embraces these three elements:

1. Opportunities for safe practice and safe failure

2. Assessment that is sensitive to both practice and performance

3. Feedback that is . . . unbalanced

Opportunities for Safe Practice and Safe Failure

Organizational theorist Peter Senge reflects on "safe practice" in the context of a baseball team's practice field on a warm summer day. He contends that "learning often occurs best . . . through interactions in a practice field where it is safe to experiment and reflect."[3] Visualize a group of children or adults on a baseball diamond, some warming up to pitch, others warming up to bat, still others throwing and catching over and over again. There is focus, precision, and a pursuit of excellence on a practice field, but there is no scorekeeping. There are no yelling fans, frantic coaches, or competition. There is simply practice and reflection, practice and reflection, both individually and in groups.

When we think of the EF-Smart Classroom, we can easily adopt the concept of safe practice fields where there are no grades for practice activities, where group work takes the pressure off individual performance, and individual work simplifies the skills needed for group work. In short, the full "game" of thinking and learning can be practiced in a way that feels safe for all learners.

How might this look in your classroom? What activities could be considered practices versus performances?

With opportunities for feedback without scores or grades on practice work, students become more open to trying new things, pushing their skills further, thinking outside the box, and taking important cognitive risks. In addition, working memory opens up due to increased automaticity, and EF skills are enhanced.

Once we introduce scores to these practice fields, the game changes. Students shift to access their most finely honed skills, sidestepping the emerging ones. They may shortcut group work if there are weak members, and they set their goals on the finish line. Though these latter skills may be important for *performance,* they are in conflict with *learning* and should be used judiciously.

The EF-Smart Classroom cultivates success for all by including both practice sessions and "game days." It includes practice and performance, informal feedback and formal grades—each tailored to the specific learning tasks and students involved.

Assessment That Is Sensitive to Both Practice and Performance

There is no shortage of books about evaluation that can help with the details of formal and informal assessment. For our purposes here, we highlight rubrics as a very powerful form of feedback for enhancing executive functioning, one that can capture both formal and informal assessment detail in a clear and transparent way.

If you don't already have a range of rubrics available to you, you may want to access RubiStar online (rubistar.4teachers .org). It is a Department of Education site designed to help build effective rubrics as well as store samples from others.

When you are employing rubrics, we recommend that you work with categories without points or scores when assessing emerging skills, and add points when students begin to work toward their final performance or product. We've added a very simple rubric to the end of this chapter (Figure 3.1) to help you assess your own work in terms of the EF-Smart Classroom—note that there are no points!

Feedback That Is . . . Unbalanced!

Yes, we like an imbalance of positives to negatives. Consider the following approaches.

All Positives   I (Margaret) attended a writer's workshop that was designed to improve and clarify the writer's "voice." The workshop consisted of four morning sessions, with lots of afternoon time devoted to exploring one's writing, or Martha's Vineyard, if we preferred. On the first day of class, we wrote rough drafts for fifteen minutes each and then were asked to give each other feedback. The only requirement was that all the comments had to be positive. Being a seasoned educator, I heard warning bells going off in my head, but they subsided as I chose to be content with the fact that even though my writing might not get much better that week, I would certainly feel good about it. Wrong.

Well, I did feel good about myself, but my writing actually improved dramatically. In fact, each person's writing had improved substantially by the end of our four days together. What had happened? For me, it was a very subtle but powerful shift toward recognizing my strengths: when we went around the room and each person explained what he or she liked specifically about my writing, I would think to myself, "Hmm! You liked that? That was easy for me—I do that all the time. I guess I'll do more of it tomorrow and see what you think . . ."

Apparently, doing more of what we already do well . . . makes us better.

Four-to-One Feedback   There is research and practice to support that for us to improve behavior in adults or children (including learning behaviors), we need to offer four positive comments to each critical one. Four to one—that's a tough ratio to hit. But, as the story of "all positives" shows, it relies on the power of positive feedback that is *specific* to create change— four days of "good job" would not have improved anyone's writing! Although it's not always possible to achieve that four-to-one ratio, most of us need to inch away from the one-to-four ratio that we often utilize in busy situations. And before we start trying to defend our practice, we must realize that "advice" often feels like criticism, especially to adolescents.

Rubrics with "Givens"   In the same spirit as the four-to-one feedback approach, perhaps we should write our rubrics (or tests) with plenty of "givens." In other words, if we design the first few items to be simple or readily doable, such that every student can succeed, imagine the effect it would have on students who are low in confidence. Not only would they earn points and gain confidence right at the beginning of an assessment, but the reduction in anxiety would actually free up more working memory. Increased working memory improves access to long-term memory and helps students both "find" and demonstrate their understanding.

Planning

We need to think carefully about the EF demands inherent in the different learning tasks and assessments we provide for our students. Some are fairly simple, well organized, and self-guiding ("filling in the blank" or copying lists of words). Others are more complex and require more organization and self-monitoring by the student (projects, papers, and group work). Another consideration is that some of our assignments are cognitively challenging (introducing new abstract material), and others are not (reviewing work or concrete facts).

Planning Assignments with Students' Executive Load in Mind
In general, it is important to remember that the more challenging the content is, the lower the executive challenge should be. So if we want to examine the abstract themes of two different stories, its best to use a simple graphic template to organize the concepts. A five-paragraph essay would be awfully difficult

for many students if they needed to analyze and synthesize brand-new information at the same time without a template.

Conversely, if we are asking our students to work with more concrete or familiar content, we may be able to utilize more challenging formats (projects or group work).

This is not to say that we cannot introduce complex abstract information in challenging formats. We just need to be clear about the kind of cognitive and EF challenges we're presenting and be ready to provide lots of support.

If we'd like our students to manage more and more complex formats, we can introduce those formats in simpler forms and then scaffold them to include greater and greater format or content challenges. Again, we need to be prepared to support those individuals who will struggle on this important EF journey. (See Chapter Four for more on this.)

Managing Timeframes with Executive Functioning in Mind

It's safe to assume that due dates that are far away just don't register on many students' radar. Or if the due date is noted on the following weeks in a planner that requires turning a page, it's basically invisible. We need to find ways to keep those dates visible and break down projects into smaller chunks until students are able to track long-term goals themselves.

This is not "enabling," and our students are not necessarily immature; it may be that they have not had sufficient instruction or enough repetitive experiences to manage this routine alone. Once we have taught students how to manage longer chunks of time, we can begin to deconstruct the scaffold we've provided them and watch them perform not only successfully but independently. We will provide examples of how this process might vary for different age groups later in this chapter.

Strategy Training

Although we like strategy training (SQ3R, for example), we find it most useful in small doses. The problem with it is that the training itself requires a significant amount of working memory, long-term memory, initiation, monitoring, and application to novel situations. In short, these strategies require a lot of executive skills in order for students to internalize and apply them. That said, we do believe that some strategies, such as mnemonic devices, work really well as an intermediate step toward independence. See Chapter Six and the Four-Quadrant Model for more on when and how to use strategies for students who need more individualized help.

Classroom Routines

We can use carefully designed routines to order and organize almost anything, but the EF-Smart Classroom is designed to ensure that routines are wrapped around a child's most challenging EF tasks: planning, initiating, sustaining, monitoring, and task completion. We like to categorize these elements using classroom-friendly terms: entry routines, transition routines, instructional routines, and routines for projects and studying for tests. We know that this list is by no means exhaustive—and you may have other routines that you like—but it's important to remember that routines should be used sparingly and judiciously to shape instructional flow without crushing it. If we don't want our classrooms to be too unstructured or too stifled, we need to find a balance of routines that work.

Entry Routines

"How should I enter the classroom?" This may seem like a silly question at first, but it is one that few teachers answer clearly for their students despite the teachers' expectations for them. We find that teachers who do make their expectations explicit get what they wish for: their students enter the room happily and are able to initiate work more effectively and with much less distraction.

That said, there is no one way to set routines, but we will give three examples to fire your imagination. Feel free to use one you like, but as in all teaching, the routine(s) you choose should reflect your own priorities and personality and the classroom you're planning for in order to be authentic and successful.

What we like most about the entry routines by Teachers A, B and C that we describe here is that they are simple, they create a predictable series of "first moves," and they reduce the EF demands inherent in transitions.

Teacher A: Primary Grades 1–3 "Good morning." Teacher A greets her students at the door and shakes hands with each as they enter (making it personal). She waits for a return squeeze of the hand and some level of eye contact before looking to the next student (ensuring connection). If she has begun the year carefully with this routine, each student will go to his cubby, unpack his bag, turn in his homework folder to the homework basket, and go directly to the circle of chairs or rug to wait for circle time to begin (the routine).

If the teacher has arranged the classroom furniture well, she can see the cubbies from the door, as well as the rug or circle, so she can monitor flow and behavior from her position (monitoring the routine). Perhaps she used an assistant or parent earlier in the year to help the students develop this routine. If so, she was careful that her assistant did not unpack the bags for the students or put their homework folder in the basket for them. Each student needs to walk through this set of steps himself in order to create an internal routine that physically and cognitively takes him from the door to the first activity space in one smooth series. These important entry steps shift the actions from those that require decision making to those that are automatic and routine, thereby reducing the load on the executive functions, particularly working memory.

Teacher B: Middle School "Good afternoon." Teacher B greets each student as he stands at the front of the room, with a clear view of the door and the desks (making it personal and monitoring the routine). He is not shuffling papers or going over plans; rather he greets each student with good eye contact (ensuring connection) and a clear voice. "It's good to see you," he might add. "Please take out materials for warm-ups—I'm eager to get started."

This simple greeting makes the human connection students crave and leads them verbally toward the first task. This teacher begins each class with a warm-up in math by having students do a quick and simple problem set that is designed for success for each student. If the warm-up is not already in the students' binders, the teacher has a routine for handing out the sheets as efficiently as possible. If personal whiteboards are available, they might use these instead as they prepare to get into that day's instruction (the routine).

Again, this simple routine is an explicit way of letting all students know what steps are expected of them as they enter the classroom, and turns a series of potential decisions into automatic routines that demand very little of executive functioning. And the fewer the decisions around these sorts of mundane moves, the more effective the instructional time and the fewer the opportunities for missteps.

Teacher C: High School or College   "Hello," Teacher C calls from the lab tables as the students enter the room. "Join me for our lab!" (making it personal and directing the flow to her location). Materials are set at the table, or students know to find their drawers of materials to bring to the tables (organization). They have been instructed earlier in the year to take out their lab books and a pen, open these books to a new page, and date the page as soon as the lab begins. Once everyone has these out, the teacher gives brief instructions and asks the students to check with their partners to be certain they are clear about the directions. She sets a timer for this activity (framing the time allotted) and asks them to begin. She wanders to each pair of students to be certain they've gotten off to the right start, asking them to review their directions if they haven't (the routine).

Like our other entry routines, this one is designed for simplicity, predictability, and a smooth transition into instruction. Students know what to expect and can focus on learning with fewer EF demands and a greater sense of competence and confidence. In addition to providing clarity and EF support, the right entry routine assures the student that the teacher is in charge and that the focus of their time together will be on learning.

Transition Routines

Transitions are hard. They are difficult for all of us because the act of ending our work flow and initiating in a new direction shifts our balance, our energy, and our attention from a familiar state to a novel one. Despite this challenge, some teachers seem to manage even the most chaotic parts of the class day well, whereas others find themselves and their students spending an excessive amount of time and energy on moving from one activity to the next.

How do good classroom managers do it? They use routines to guide their transitions. We'll review those routines here and highlight those that help with the most difficult parts of the school day: the beginning and the end of the day or class. Transitions are difficult for students because they cause everything to shift: the physical space, the teacher's tone of voice, her choice of words, her speed of movement, and the students' choices about doing what they want versus doing what they are told.

The entry routines described in the previous section help address the important shift at the beginning of the day or class period. But what about the end? Isn't it much easier to simply let go of the structure and expectations and dismiss students? Yes, if our expectations for our students end as soon as they walk out the door.

However, if there are expectations for hallway behavior, homework, or projects, the EF demands continue and may even increase at this juncture. When they leave us, we are no longer there to guide them. Our students face independent organization, planning, initiating, and monitoring, often while suffering from low blood sugar and some degree of fatigue.

Just as "going to bed" routines help even adults to end the day, our "end of the day" classroom routines can provide comfort, direction, and closure for our students.

The Reminder   All good closing routines begin with a reminder:

"You have ten minutes left to finish your team work and clean up."

"Please watch the clock; we will spend the last five minutes closing together."

"Once we've finished this part of the lesson, you will spend the last five minutes writing a headline to summarize your thoughts."

Reminders are important because they allow the student to begin the internal shift needed in order to manage the transition smoothly. If we suddenly end class declaring that the students are out of time, they don't know what to do with the flow they had going. Some students actually experience irritation and confusion when faced with such a sudden change in flow, which immediately robs them of the ability to process, organize, or take in additional input. It's almost 100 percent certain that those last few words we throw at their backs as they fly out the door will miss their mark!

Open Your Planners   After working in schools and clinical settings for years, we are convinced that planners are *the most essential tools* for capturing and organizing work and for managing the executive skills related to homework, projects, and studying for tests. Not having a planner is equivalent to showing up at a bike race without a course map—there's a really good chance of getting lost unless you tail someone pretty closely. In either event, the lesson learned is that tailing someone is essential: independent performance is not going to work.

So it is essential to have a planner, whether paper or electronic, every day, in every class, with every teacher, and to spend time at the end of each class marking in it. Using a planner frees up the working memory portion of executive functioning, allowing students to access more important, higher-level thinking in class. It reduces anxiety too.

There are three simple steps for using a planner effectively. First, when there are three to five minutes left in class, ask all students to take out their planners and record the assignments and materials needed. Even if assignments are posted online, that will neither help the student get out of the building at the end of the day with all the necessary materials nor ensure that actual *planning* has taken place. Second, if you have announced a test or long-term assignment—even if there is a detailed assignment sheet or study guide—ask students to mark the due date in their planners *sideways* (so that it doesn't look like their daily work). Third, ask students to assign themselves work and study days leading up to that date. In some settings, we award one point for each of these planner "moves," marking students' points on that day's planner page and making the routine even more concrete. Three points for the day ensures success for both the day and the week!

For a more detailed description of how we like to set up and work with planners, see the section titled Planners in Chapter Four.

Long Closings   Some teachers like to build a long closing into their classroom routines, which allows students to reflect and to organize their thoughts and materials. Activities during these extended closings can take the form of working on journal entries or lab notes, doing cleanup routines, or even beginning homework in class.

To enhance classroom culture and bring the session to a quiet close, some teachers read to their students from a work of fiction or nonfiction that pertains to the focus of their current study. If set up right, this strategy is both instructive and relaxing, as students recline a bit in their seats to listen or even close their eyes. This moment of pause in the midst of a busy learning environment allows everyone not only to shift his or her "flow" but also to process and internalize the learning that just went on. For a similar reason, some teachers end the day or class period with deep breathing or simple stretches.

In this busy multitasking world we live in, teachers can sometimes come to believe that the more information they cram into a chunk of time, the more learning takes place. Not true. Not just students but all of us need time to pause, reflect, and download new information. A longer closing provides this time.

Transitions Between Activities   For many students, even the transitions between activities can be challenging. Again, the idea of interrupting flow and changing direction can be unsettling. With simple "transitional moves," we can help even the most reactive student.

- If we are working with a timer for an activity, this is a natural reminder to students that change is pending.

- If we have their materials generally organized in baskets, desks, or folders, a simple reminder to pull those out or put them away will signal the beginning of a transition.

- Some teachers choose to stand in a certain place in the classroom (for example, by the door or at the front of the room) to signal that a change will begin.

- Other teachers like to dim the lights as a gentle signal for change.

Any of these and more will work—as long as the signal is consciously designed and applied with consistency and kindness.

Instructional Routines

The routines we've highlighted so far are the ones that frame the school day or class period. The ones that follow frame the lesson itself. Many of these are simple research-based techniques that are discussed in detail in other texts. We describe them here because we believe that it is the conscious patterning and timing of these techniques that affect the EF challenges of our instruction.

In general, the ideal lesson will require most if not all of the following elements to optimize learning and manage the challenges of executive functioning.

Warm-ups We like warm-ups—a lot—for the very reasons we've described earlier: they provide practice, focus, predictability, and success for all students. That they enhance a smooth transition just adds to their effectiveness. In addition, the research is very clear that regular practice brings skills to a level of automaticity that dramatically reduces the need for working memory in learning new information. If math facts, fluency practices in reading, or verb conjugations in Spanish are rehearsed regularly, those skills become chunked as single automatic "scripts," which can be blended with new information, utilizing less cognitive energy.

Most subject areas or units of study have elements that can be turned into practice sets (for example, editing sentences, plugging variables into simple equations, reviewing the scientific method or lab routines), and it's important to turn some of these into warm-ups.

Review and Preview   An effective lesson follows warm-ups with "review and preview." This is designed to be a short review of the major concepts that were covered in the previous lesson, linked very consciously to the major concepts in the current day's lesson. For example: "Yesterday we talked about how settlers created committees to help govern their early villages, and today we will talk about how those committees banded together to create larger, more formal groups we now call government." Reviewing "re-minds" students by having them access the concepts they've been building in their long-term memory; previewing extends this and creates a place for new information to land in an organized way.

Although this is a quick and simple instructional move, *it is essential* for ordering the higher-level concepts and EF skills involved in learning. This step *cannot* be skipped.

New Material   Learning new material is the greatest challenge in education—yet it is what we crave as learners and devote most of our time to. If the setup has been done well, this is the most cognitively exciting part of learning. If the setup is loose or nonexistent, it can be one of the most challenging and potentially frustrating.

In addition to reviewing, previewing, and warming up, the most important things to remember in presenting new material are to

- Keep it organized—use unit planners and lesson plans to manage your own flow of information, and design materials that visually demonstrate the main points and subpoints. Many teachers find that when they design handouts in landscape rather than portrait format, they reduce the amount of information presented at one time, which makes the task more manageable.

- Present information in manageable chunks (depending on the age of the students)—most of us like to process only three points at a time, and certainly no more than five.

- Offer frequent opportunities for reflection and review—provide opportunities for discussion, application, or practice after presenting those three to five points.

Application   For our purposes here, we will describe application as the opportunity to take new information and apply it in a new or personal way. This can be as simple as a discussion, a worksheet, a chart, or a drawing. Whatever form it takes, a good application activity requires the student to explore understandings more deeply, examine their misunderstandings, and question important aspects of the new material. So when we're teaching about the concept of perspective in painting, for example, students would process this more deeply if they were asked to create a drawing using perspective. And then perhaps they could apply the concepts in a new way or review the work of others in the class. This very dynamic reflective learning not only challenges students' executive functioning but also creates important pathways that will be needed later in order for students to access information. Without depth of processing, eventual understanding and performances may be scattered, shallow, or transient.

Review   In order to support and strengthen the learning that occurs each day, the ideal lesson ends with review—this can be done through discussion, application, or practice. This final opportunity to reconsider the concepts, skills, and information allows students to retrace important pathways one more time and contributes to feelings of familiarity and confidence, positive emotions that keep students open to new learning and allow them to take cognitive risks with their uncertain initial emerging understandings.

Routines for Projects and Studying for Texts

The "smartest" routines for projects and studying for tests begin with the planner! As we described earlier, using the planner to mark deadlines and work days has the immediate effect of reducing anxiety, freeing up working memory, and creating an effective road map.

Projects   Long-term projects should be introduced with a detailed, visually simple assignment sheet that lays out the important steps needed to complete the assignment. We believe that by designing these with bulleted points rather than with wordy paragraphs, you're creating a document that will be "cognitively friendly" to the widest range of learners. We also like each bulleted item to have a check-off box on the side that students can use to monitor their progress along the route to completion.

If the project involves partners or teams, you should include additional sheets that outline when and how to interact. For older students, this plan may be more of a template that groups can use to plan their meetings and steps together.

Remember, there is a fine line between effective detail and overwhelming detail. If the assignment sheet includes more than five important elements, there's a good chance that students will attach a feeling of anxiety to it that could last throughout the entire project. If it is initially presented with more than three pages, the internalized student response will most likely be fight or flight!

Studying for Tests   We group our discussion of studying for tests with that for projects because they both pull heavily on *independent implementation of all the EF skills*, from organizing and prioritizing to initiating, sustaining, monitoring, and task completion. A glitch in any one of these can derail the entire effort.

As with projects, preparing for tests requires teachers to create a good review sheet. Students should be directed to highlight the $10 words on their review sheets and make effective use of their planners. They are taught to post the due date sideways in the planner and schedule study days. (See Chapter Four for details and a visual.)

One of the most interesting parts of this exercise is to watch how differently students will plan the number and timing of their study days. Some students need two days for foreign language but four for history exams. Younger students may need five days to prepare for a spelling test but almost none for literature reviews.

Regardless of their final determinations, the mere act of making this decision taps deeply into students' perception of both the task and their own study skills. This is a deep and important step in developing and internalizing EF skills, as there are few tasks that demand this level of reflection and prioritization. Repeated opportunities to revisit and build these skills with guidance enhances both competence and automaticity in an area of planning that even some adults never master.

This same task of using the planner to prompt forethought and reflection can be applied to the student's study plan for different courses. Studying for math clearly requires different strategies than studying for history or science or literature. Aside from these subject-matter differences, each teacher's expectations and style of assessment will determine the kind of studying needed for each assessment.

The best way to approach studying for tests is to be very clear about how to prepare for a specific assessment each time, being careful to promote depth of understanding over rote knowledge. (This is very important if our goals are aimed at learning, not just grades.) Once students understand how to study for an assessment, it is vitally important to revisit the idea that each assessment is different and requires different strategies. A brief discussion contrasting how the current assessment differs from a previous one will highlight this idea. It is this point of considering the contrast and applying that information that will bring students to higher levels of executive functioning.

Beyond planning to study, the act of studying has its own subroutines. Depending on the student's energies and sensibilities, study periods may be short or long, restful or active, independent or shared. (See the Planners section in Chapter Four for more specific subroutines.) Whichever study strategies students choose, in order to maximize their EF skills, their study sessions should as much as possible be guided by their planner, involve repetition, be appropriately timed according to their age and energy levels, and pursued in a positive frame of mind. Now we are employing all four of the tune-up tools mentioned at the beginning of the chapter!

In this section, we looked at how both teacher and student routines rely on the tools of conscious planning, repetition, time, and frame of mind. In the next section, we discuss the design of the physical setup to support both the concepts of classroom culture and effective routines.

Classroom Design

We finish with classroom design as a very concrete way to support executive skills and optimize the flow of routines.

Furniture Arrangement and Organization of Materials

Furniture setup is the first clue students receive about the day's work as they enter a classroom. Will they be working in groups at tables, individually with their teacher as leader, or in some combination of both?

Just as we ask our students to organize their materials in order to make efficient use of their time and cognitive energy, we need to organize classroom furniture and materials to optimize instruction and practice.

As we stand at the door and look around, we should ask ourselves a few questions:

- Does the classroom organization send a message of order and easy accessibility? Are the desks clustered purposefully or lined up evenly? Are current books and materials within reach? Are others stored away?

- Does the furniture enhance or detract from classroom flow during transitions? Are there clear paths for student movement?

- Are there times when the furniture and materials should be moved around?

- Is the order within the room explicitly discussed to further enhance accessibility and efficient use, or is it a bit of a mystery?

Although there is literature devoted to room arrangement, for our purposes here, suffice it to say that your students form an expectation of your lesson and their day as soon as they walk into the room, and their attention and productivity are enhanced by purposeful organization. If you want to streamline the EF demands of a lesson, be sure that your furniture and spaces reflect the kind of instruction and work your students will be involved with that day. And when you change the furniture around, you can change their expectations. (After one particularly challenging semester, I [Margaret] rearranged the furniture as a concrete sign and reminder that things were going to be different!)

Walls
There are lots of varying opinions on how bright and busy our classroom wall spaces should be. You may not be surprised to read, however, that in order to enhance executive functioning, any information posted on the walls should have a meaningful reference to the most essential work and organization that

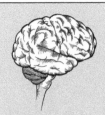

Brain Alert!

Viewing nature and drinking a glass of lemonade. These are two of the newest and perhaps most exciting recommendations we've heard about lately, as they rely on simple activities that many of us enjoy.

In new research on attention, Kaplan and Berman report that viewing nature or walking in nature for as little as twenty minutes per week provides just the right level of cognitive input, or "soft fascination" as they refer to it, to allow our brains to recalibrate to a more restful level of executive functioning and self-regulation.* This restful level seems to last well beyond the time spent in nature and has brought about dramatic long-term effects in some of the subjects studied.

Kaplan and Berman also discuss the role of glucose depletion during intensive working memory tasks. Their study showed that a serving of lemonade was enough to restore those depleted levels. This research suggests that we should allow students snack breaks. Some of our high school students start school long before their bodies can think about eating breakfast. By midmorning, they would surely benefit from some glucose!

*Kaplan, S., and Berman, M. G. "Directed Attention as a Common Resource for Executive Functioning and Self-Regulation." *Perspectives on Psychological Science*, 2010, 5(1), 43–57.

takes place in the room. Remember, visual information is a powerful draw, so posting a few common routines or rules will support executive functioning, whereas crowding the walls with pictures and other nonessential visuals will compete. If you do like to display student work and inspirational posters, perhaps find a place at the back or side of the room where student focus during instruction is not an issue.

PLANNING FOR CHANGE

It is certainly an understatement to say that this chapter covers a wide range of recommendations! As you use this book for your own purposes, however, what is most important is that you reflect on *your own* classroom and *your own* student challenges and areas of need, then begin to pinpoint which elements in your daily routines effectively support EF skills in your classroom and which do not.

We offer a simple rubric (Figure 3.1) to help you reflect on your classroom and move toward creating the most supportive environment possible. Remember that as much for yourself as for your students, planning, time, repetition, and mind-set will help you craft the changes that will make a difference for all.

Figure 3.1   Tools and Targets for Self-Evaluation

	Effective	**Emerging**	**Not So Much**
Tools			
Planning			
Repetition			
Time			
Mind-set			
Notes to self:			
Targets			
Classroom Culture			
Planning Instruction			
Classroom Routines			
Classroom Design			
Notes to self:			

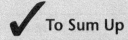 **To Sum Up**

- By understanding executive functioning, we can make shifts in our teaching structures and routines that will help all students in our classes succeed and become more independent.

- Using the tune-up tools of planning, time, repetition, and mind-set, we create the elements that allow us to flexibly adjust our classrooms and teaching practices in accordance with students' EF needs.

- By coaching our students through their EF challenges, we can guide them to success and improve their confidence.

- By attending to elements of classroom structure, we can set up our classrooms in such a way that we lead students to higher-level functioning. These elements include classroom culture, planning instruction, classroom routines, and classroom design.

? Time to Reflect

1. What classroom routines do you currently employ that support executive functioning? Do they address entries, transitions, long-term projects?

_____

_____

_____

2. When you consider your physical space, what feature most clearly maximizes executive functioning in your room? Is there a way you might change things about your furniture, your wall spaces, or your view of the outdoors?

_____

_____

_____

3. What do you like best about your classroom culture? What changes might contribute even more strongly to a positive environment?

_____

_____

_____

4. Note any other key takeaways from this chapter.

_____

_____

_____

Supporting Students Who Need More Help

4

E ven in classrooms that are EF smart, some students
have trouble managing school demands. These students need more targeted help to manage the daily
workload and to develop the routines and habits they need to
become independent learners.

The targeted strategies outlined and described in this
chapter have been used successfully in classroom settings
and learning resource centers, as well as in individual student
sessions. Although there is only limited research on specific
interventions for students with weak executive skills, we have
integrated what is available, in keeping with our support for
evidence-based practice. Incorporate your knowledge of each
specific student and your own classroom to modify these as
needed.

How do you know which behaviors to target? In most
cases, you know from your own classroom observations as
well as conversations with the student where a student is trip-
ping up. Combine this information with that of other teachers
and that gleaned from a conversation with the parents, and
you generally have your targets!

If you are unclear about the specific nature of the problem,
then you can consider requesting that a qualified staff person
in your school administer a questionnaire that assesses behaviors associated with executive functioning. There are many

such scales that are commercially available, but we prefer the Behavior Rating Inventory of Executive Functions (BRIEF) to help guide these decisions.[1] When you have questions about whether or not there are co-occurring conditions that need attention, a referral for more comprehensive evaluation may be needed. In Table 4.1, you will find a list of specific interventions for specific EF targets. The column headings are based on the core executive functions as described by Gioia and his colleagues (see Chapter One). We devote the remainder of the chapter to in-depth descriptions of each of these interventions and comments about their use.

PLANNERS

Recommended levels: unless otherwise noted, grade 2 through adult (or whenever homework, tests, or long-term projects begin in your school)

As basic as it may seem, we want to state here that the first step in using a planner is writing the student's name in bold letters on the front or back . . . just in case he loses it. The second most important step is for students to bring their planner to every class and for each teacher to give three to five precious minutes at the end of class for students to write down their assignments as illustrated in Figure 4.1. Many teachers currently post assignments online for their students, but this is not enough—many students, and especially students with certain EF challenges, can't even get out of the building at the end of the day with the materials they need to do homework that night. We joke with some parents that their children should be required to show their planner as a ticket to get into the car at the end of the day. If they don't have it, their penalty is simply . . . to go get it.

For those families who connect later in the evening after work, the reality is that when they walk through the door,

Table 4.1 Specific Interventions for Specific Targets

	Organization of Materials	Planning and Organizing	Working Memory	Task Monitoring	Task Initiation and Completion	Emotional Control
Planners						
Entries for every class, including "None"		✓	✓	✓	✓	
Long-term projects, entered sideways		✓	✓	✓	✓	
Long-term projects, workdays assigned		✓	✓	✓	✓	
1–10 confidence scale for tests		✓		✓	✓	✓
Thursday grade checks				✓		
Thursday notes to teachers		✓		✓	✓	
Sunday's weekly preview with parents		✓	✓	✓	✓	✓

(Continued)

Table 4.1 Specific Interventions for Specific Targets (*Continued*)

	Organization of Materials	Planning and Organizing	Working Memory	Task Monitoring	Task Initiation and Completion	Emotional Control
Materials						
Trapper Keeper with weekly checks	✓	✓	✓		✓	
Locker organizers with weekly checks	✓	✓	✓		✓	
Use Google Docs or email assignments to self as backup	✓	✓	✓	✓	✓	
TIGERS folder	✓	✓	✓	✓		
Reading						
Warm-up: Great Leaps		✓	✓		✓	
Warm-up: Reasoning and Reading		✓	✓			
Literary web and Inspiration software		✓	✓	✓	✓	

	Organization of Materials	Planning and Organizing	Working Memory	Task Monitoring	Task Initiation and Completion	Emotional Control
Highlighting $10 words: textbooks—subtitles and paragraphs	✓		✓	✓	✓	
Highlighting $10 words: novels and short stories with chapter summary bullets	✓	✓	✓	✓	✓	
Highlighting $10 words: assignment sheets	✓	✓	✓	✓	✓	

(Continued)

Table 4.1 Specific Interventions for Specific Targets (*Continued*)

	Organization of Materials	Planning and Organizing	Working Memory	Task Monitoring	Task Initiation and Completion	Emotional Control
Writing						
Warm-up: seven-minute writing samples			✓		✓	
Organizing: Inspiration software		✓	✓	✓	✓	
Checking your work: COPS		✓	✓	✓	✓	
Checking your work: *Learning Grammar Through Writing*		✓	✓	✓	✓	
Math						
Warm-up: aplusmath.com; blank times table; triangular flash cards			✓		✓	
Show all your work		✓	✓	✓		
Guided practice			✓		✓	

Student Planner   1-10 ☐

	Monday	Tuesday	Wednesday	Thursday	Friday	Saturday • Sunday
English	Ø	☑ Read Chap. 2	___ PREP GRAPHIC	GRAPHIC DUE		
Math	☑ Pg. 47 # 1-10 odd	Bring eg. of an equation ___ Study	Study	Study	TEST	
Science	Bring a cup of dirt!	Ø				
Social Studies	☑ Read article	☑ Journal response				
			Grandma's birthday	* THURSDAY NOTE		

Figure 4.1   Sample Student Planner Page

their children may be watching TV claiming that they finished the homework, but with no planner at home. We like to make it a rule that if they neglect to bring their planner home, they lose electronic privileges or another important privilege as a way of learning the importance of bringing the planner home daily. We ask parents to do this in a teaching sort of way, not punitively: "Oh, that's too bad. I'm afraid you have lost your electronic privileges for today. Fortunately, you will have a chance to earn them back tomorrow—just bring your planner home. In the meantime, how can you double-check on your assignments for tonight?"

In schools that do not give out homework, the planner can be a great visible way to track in-school projects and work.

Entries for Every Class, Including "None"

In every class, every day, it's important for students to write down each assignment given or to write "None." It doesn't really matter whether they write "None" or the null sign or a big X, but it is important that at the end of the day when students are packing up, they can glance at their planner and see very clearly what they need for homework so that they bring home the right materials. The word "None" tells them very clearly that there really was no assignment given in that class that day—they did not forget to write down an assignment. In planners that get signed to ensure accuracy, this also confirms for the parent that the teacher agrees that there is nothing to be done for that subject.

Some students also need to add a check box to some assignments to remind themselves to bring home materials.

These may seem like small details, but when students have been disorganized and unsuccessful for years, they need the confidence that these small strategies bring to help them feel positive about their work and their chances for success each day.

Long-Term Projects, Entered Sideways

Most assignments are designed to be turned in the next day, but many complex and meaningful projects require more time. Although these kinds of projects allow students to choose more personal topics and responses, they represent the most difficult executive management challenges in school. We suggest that to mark long-term assignments and tests differently in the planner, students should write them in *sideways, on the due date*.

Long-Term Projects, Workdays Assigned

Immediately after entering long-term assignments and test dates, students should enter their project workdays in their planner as regular assignments. To do this effectively, students will have to ask themselves some questions:

1. Do I need a brainstorming day?

2. Do I need to assign myself "final draft work" the day before it's due?

3. Will some of the work be done in class?

4. Will I have to find dates when I can work with others?

5. How many workdays will I need for this particular project?

6. Will I need to work on a weekend?

7. Have I built in an extra day for the unexpected?

At first, students may need to be guided through each of these questions, but over time, and with repetition, they should begin to ask (and answer) many of them automatically. You may find, however, that without consistent practice, students will continue to require help every time.

1–10 Confidence Scale for Tests

Recommended levels: grade 5 through adult

Students need to plan for tests in much the same way that they plan for long-term assignments: they should mark the due dates sideways in their planners and assign themselves study days. However, tests provide an additional challenge for students: many don't know how to determine "when they're ready" or "when they've studied enough." Consequently, they may spend the wrong amount of time, energy, or attention on the task. We recommend that students be guided to ask themselves, "On a scale of 1 to 10, how ready am I for this test?" On this scale, 1 represents "I don't understand the material at all," and 10 means "I can ace this test!" Generally we find that when students give themselves an 8 or 9, they're fairly ready for the test.

Why did we include the confidence scale in the section on planners, you ask? It's because not all students are good at predicting their readiness, especially at first. So we're recommending that, once students have finished some study, they enter their "confidence number" in their planners to check for readiness. If their number is low, they know to study more. If high, they know they can move on. An interesting addition to this strategy is to get students to enter the actual grade they receive on that test in that same space to identify whether they had been overconfident or underconfident. If they rated their confidence at 8 and received an 80 percent, then they are right on! If they receive a 70 or 90 percent, we consider that to be fairly accurate too. Surprisingly, students are generally accurate within a point, so when you find those who are far off, it will be worth taking a closer look at them in terms of their confidence, anxiety, or ability to self-reflect.

Like some of the other strategies, this small step may make the difference between anxiety and confidence, success or failure. It is a strategy with long-term payoff because it teaches a system for self-monitoring and teaches a reflective approach to task management.

Thursday Grade Checks

Recommended levels: grade 5 through adult

Some students have an inflated sense of how well they're doing in terms of grades. After all, they might be popular, have parents who adore them, or live in a sunny climate— apparently things are going well, they like to assume. So, not to burst their bubble but to introduce reality gently, we do Thursday grade checks. How would they otherwise know that they're missing assignments? Answer: they wouldn't. So for them to succeed, they need to be aware that they sometimes miss things and need a backup system to check up on themselves. The process is simple—on Thursdays we check grades in every class. You can do this online or one-on-one with the student.

Why Thursdays? We have found that when students are not being realistic about their work or grades, they may be missing some work or turning in low-quality work during the week. In that case, if they find this out on a Thursday, they can schedule a time to finish their work before the weekend, or work on it over the weekend. Although we believe that some students can and should have reduced assignments, we do not believe that it's a good idea just to let late or incomplete assignments go. This gives students the mistaken impression that work (or problems) will just go away if they ignore them. But rather than trying to fit all this work into the school week, many students can manage their time better if they finish up over the weekend. As a bonus, we've heard more than one student exclaim—yes, actually *exclaim*—that they are downright happy to be heading to school on Monday ALL CAUGHT UP and organized. We know—they don't always look like they care, but most often they do!

Thursday Notes to Teachers

Recommended levels: grade 5 through high school

What's with the Thursdays? Same principle: it gives students time to make up work before the new week begins. Thursday notes to teachers are simply this: the student, after checking her grades, and often with the help of an adult, writes a polite note to her teacher(s) stating, "My work is all caught up, and I have received all passing grades this week. If I am missing something, please let me know so I can make it up over the weekend."

The purpose of this strategy is for students to self-reflect, self-advocate, and, ultimately, take responsibility for the work. Research has shown that effective intervention for students with weak organizational skills includes discussions to facilitate planning. Thursday notes help the student learn the importance of having a backup plan to compensate for the fact that he sometimes is unaware of what he is missing. Thus Thursday notes highlight the value of plans and facilitate accurate self-evaluation.

We recommend that an adult help with the writing at first, as many students just don't know how to put these thoughts into words; they seem to know that there is such a thing as a "polite letter," but most just don't know how to begin to write it. Once the student has written a sample Thursday note, she can save it to be reused each week. Again, although it might not seem so at first, most students appreciate our help with this.

Sunday's Weekly Preview with Parents

Recommended levels: grade 5 through high school

Ah, something for the parents to do! When we can enlist their help in previewing the plan for the week, the opportunities for modeling and reinforcing planning skills grow. Because our work with executive strategies and habits have as much to do with the "real world" as they do with school, this strategy is unique in the way it allows students to generalize their skills outside of the school building and to recognize that even parents need organizational skills.

On Sundays (preferably after a good meal), parents should sit down with their children, open their calendars and planners together, and map out the week. Clearly, this gives the strong message that *everyone* has to plan and organize, and it also allows the student to see what is coming up in his or her week. If Grandma is having a birthday dinner on Wednesday, then studying for that Thursday test might need to happen on Tuesday. Or if there is an away football game on Monday, it's best to assume that not much else will get done that night.

These sorts of things tend to "pop up" on students and thwart their otherwise good intentions to get work done. And too much "thwarting" can cause students to eventually give up, feeling that no matter how hard they try, they can't seem to succeed. With the right planning, however, students do improve, and their success becomes contagious. In fact, at times there are parents who appreciate the nudge . . .

MATERIALS

Planners are so important that we have given them a section of their own. However, there are additional materials that support students' EF skills.

Trapper Keeper with Weekly Checks

Recommended levels: grade 3 through high school

(In grades 1 through 3, the structure is provided by the EF-smart classroom itself. This is part of the reason that EF problems don't always show up until later.)

For those students who have trouble with organization of materials, Trapper Keepers (or some other such large binder system) help tremendously in getting them through the day. With it, they are able to keep all notebooks, folders, pencil bags, and planners in one place. Without it, many students tend to "leave parts of themselves" all over the school building. Although some teachers have strong feelings about having individual binders for their classes, it may be important to temper that preference with the benefits that a one-binder system can provide. This is a simple accommodation to make when needed. Carrying a backpack to every class can work well also—this can be decided based on the general culture of the school.

Whether a student uses a large single binder system, a large Trapper Keeper, or a backpack, most often he will need to do a "clean-out" session about once per week to keep the papers inside organized. It is important that the clean-out be done by student hands and with student decision making. Otherwise, the internal microdecisions that need to be made are made by the adult rather than the student—the adult improves his or her executive functioning while the student gets better at following micromanaged directions. The parent's or adult's role is to remind the student that it's time to check for organization, gently coach him through this work if he gets stuck, and provide positive and specific feedback for small jobs well done. Once a good routine for putting away materials is established, the weekly check may not be needed. Until then, make it a Friday date!

Locker Organizers with Weekly Checks

Recommended levels: grade 6 through high school

If your school has lockers, it will be just as important to teach some students how to organize these as it is to organize binders. Parents and teachers sometimes make the mistake of organizing a locker for the student, but this can work against them: it's not the organized product that's important but the decision making and the act of organizing that internalize this skill for students. That said, if a student is just exhausted from a week of school demands, it's certainly all right to give him or her a hand.

Use Google Docs or Email Assignments to Self as a Backup

Recommended levels: middle school through adult

Losing completed assignments can be an overwhelmingly frustrating part of a student's school day! And when it's a long-term project or paper, it can be utterly defeating. Yet this is what some students with EF difficulties face every day and week. To prevent these losses, some of the older students we've worked with have found a way to foolproof their disorganization: at their home or public library, they work on Google Docs to create files that are shared with their teachers, they email their assignments to themselves in addition to making hard copies, or they save their work in Dropbox. This way, if they leave their work on the kitchen table or on the bus, they can quietly print out another copy at school. Crisis averted, face saved.

TIGERS (Take Initiative: Get Everything Ready for School!) Folders

Recommended levels: grades 1 through 3

For the early grades, teachers often help students become organized and remain organized by using special homework folders. These are usually one bright color (often yellow) for everyone, and students are instructed to place daily work in one pocket and homework in the other, or to put work to go home in one pocket and ongoing work in the other. However you decide to organize it, be sure to be consistent and remember that you need to allot time for organizing it every day. Some teachers even use acronyms to label these folders—our favorite is TIGERS: it reminds the student to Take Initiative: Get Everything Ready for School!

We've noticed that as students move into the upper grades and require more complex binder systems for organization, some hang on to that idea of keeping homework in a front pocket just as they did with their earlier TIGERS or homework folders.

READING

Reading is a joyful activity for many students, yet for those with EF problems, their struggle with processing layers of information may be so profound that they are unable to read for pleasure, or effectively for information. Some of these students are actually identified as having reading disabilities, and some are referred for reading comprehension tests over and over again with no clear outcome.

The problem with reading and executive functioning is not always rooted in the decoding process. Often it has much more to do with the *efficiency* of students' decoding and their ability to stack layers of meaningful information found in longer text. If you think about it, each paragraph holds meaning that is separate from the ones around it. In fact, so does each sentence and each subsection in a textbook. Yet these students often attack reading as a task that requires "collecting" single words while layering them with the question, "How long will this take?" With low efficiency and poor cognitive organization, many students give up or have to overrely on others to help them pull meaning from text.

The following are several strategies that help students build automaticity, mental organization, and a more active, engaged approach to comprehending text.

Reading Warm-ups

We like warm-ups for academic skills! Think about warming up for a sport, perhaps basketball. You know there is a complex game later in the week that requires dribbling, shooting, passing, plays, and lots of defense, but you don't practice the sport by playing that complex game at each practice. You begin each practice with brief, isolated warm-ups—dribbling, running, shooting, and passing. These are the simple elements of the game that require automaticity so that you're able to perform them without conscious thought. In terms of working memory, these become chunked as "scripts" or routines that you access as a single fluid thought. This "frees up RAM" so that you can think about and perform the other elements of the sport.

Warm-ups might also be effective because they bypass some of the difficulties with working memory—for example, if I have trouble pulling up information from working memory to start a complex task, then the warm-up will have already laid the basics out in front of me, and I do not need to search for that information to start the more complex parts.

In reading, we can also have students begin with warm-ups in order to create automaticity and to free up their working memory for the more complex tasks, including predicting, comparing, contrasting, and finding the main idea and supporting detail. This is a high-level thinking challenge—fortunately the fix is easy for a large percentage of our students!

Reading Warm-up for Automaticity and Comprehension: Great Leaps
Recommended levels: kindergarten through adult

There are a variety of ways to use warm-ups to build reading automaticity, but our favorite by far is Great Leaps (see www.greatleaps.com). This program comes in a binder and requires the student to do three one-minute readings per day with an adult; the whole process takes five minutes. Because it requires one-on-one interaction, most educators we know use it in very small group settings (about three students), where each student cycles through to do a reading while the others engage in free reading or other reading work. Alternatively, some educators use volunteers at the beginning of the day to help students with this warm-up—this is the approach initially used to build the program's research base.

In Great Leaps, the student does a one-minute reading of phonic sounds ($/r/$, $/l/$, $/s/$, $/o/$, and so on), a one-minute reading of sight word *phrases* (rather than single sight words) to enhance cognitive "chunking," and a one-minute reading of paragraphs. This nicely covers the reading equivalents of dribbling, shooting, and passing. Immediately afterwards, the student reads whatever text he or she needs for school or for pleasure. Research shows that speed and comprehension improve with these simple practices. In our experience, using Great Leaps for two or three months with students who have average to above-average intelligence often improves their comprehension skills with text that is one grade level higher! Their feelings of accomplishment increase weekly as they move through the program, and their frustration level drops. With this experience of success, they will enjoy reading more.

Warm-up for Organizing and Categorizing Thoughts: The Reasoning and Reading Series
Recommended levels: grade 3 through adult

Automaticity with decoding, sight words, and paragraph reading is important, and so is knowing how to categorize information we pull from text. With practice, good readers learn to juggle those balls and add in the higher-level task of organizing their thoughts as they read.

Many students with EF problems have trouble organizing not only their planners, binders, and lockers but often also their thoughts, in regard to both incoming and outgoing information. When we look at reading, we need to consider the challenges of incoming information. The higher-level thoughts readers juggle are often about similarities and differences, sequencing, main characters, plot, theme, crisis, and the main idea and connected detail. When reading, people actually create patterns or "file folders" in their heads to hold these things for their future consideration. We have found that using a five- to ten-minute warm-up that requires sorting of simple ideas and concepts helps with this process.

Our favorite packaged materials for this kind of warm-up are the Reasoning and Reading series, published by Educator's Publishing Services (see http://eps.schoolspecialty.com/). Each page contains material that provides both the structure and the language needed to help a student identify and practice using the organizational framework embedded in stories, novels, or textbooks. It also helps them with writing and thinking, even though the series title doesn't suggest it. For example, the first section has quick pages dedicated to simply finding similarities and differences and to categorization of thought. Each book then goes on to examine sentences as single units of thought, with an emphasis on how word sequence affects meaning. It then moves on to examine paragraphs as broader categories of thought and logic. Though they may sound complex by description, the books themselves are designed with simplicity and mastery in mind. They are targeted for students in grades 3 through 8; however, students in high school or beyond could easily benefit from the cognitive structure they provide.

For those who require a more visual, concrete map of their thoughts as they read, consider using mind maps or Inspiration software, described in the next section.

Literary Web and Inspiration Software

Recommended levels: kindergarten through adult

As they begin to sort abstract features of text (setting, characterization, symbols and themes, conflict and resolution) and make decisions about them, some students will require a more visual or concrete way to store that information. Graphic organizers, such as those included in Inspiration software (see http://www.inspiration.com), are the tools that seem to work best, as they are computer based (see Figure 4.2). When teachers create these templates to include the precise elements needed in specific text, students learn, through guided repetition, to sort their ideas and save them for later consideration.

It is important to keep the elements to a minimum at first and then build as the student reaches mastery. Once they have achieved mastery, it is important for students to create their own organizational webs, beginning with the simple and then increasing the complexity. (You can find more about this technique in Chapter Six.) One of our students who had dramatically low working memory used Inspiration daily, focusing

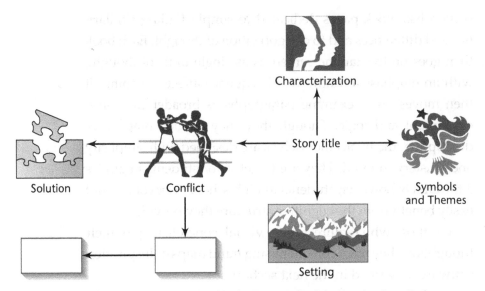

Figure 4.2 Literary Web Created with Inspiration Software

on "building three important points." Eventually, he was able to "open Inspiration in his head," picture the important elements, and name the ideas he would put in those boxes. In other words, over time, this working memory strategy became so efficient that he was able to organize his verbal input and output in real-time conversations!

Highlighting $10 Words: Engaging with Text

Recommended levels: reading levels grade 3 through adult

   (For this strategy, the student's base reading level, as opposed to academic grade placement, should be at least third grade.)

What are $10 words? We used to call these "key words," but students and teachers both struggled to know what the term meant—key to whom, and why? Because most students know the value of money and have no trouble making decisions based on money, we now call key words $10 words and ask students to find only a few, highly valuable words to highlight. Most succinctly, we ask students to "highlight the most important words . . . and it costs $10 to highlight each one!"

Now students and teachers have placed a value on finding the most important words. And there's an added benefit: not only do students highlight the most important words, but they are forced to make microdecisions about the text. In other words, students must focus, read very carefully, consider the topic, make tiny decisions, and act. (We look more specifically at highlighting textbooks, novels, and assignment sheets in the next sections.) These processes together define real reading, as they require the student to actually engage and interact with the text to make it their own. Now they're doing effective reading work!

Textbooks

Textbooks, as most authors and publishers will tell you, are organized in a very clear and conscious way. If they are well written, the main ideas are held in their titles, subtitles, and italicized vocabulary. Simple as that. If you want to know what a textbook (or magazine article or nonfiction book) is about, just read the titles and subtitles. (This strategy saved me [Margaret] more than a few times during graduate school when the reading overload was too much!)

Again, many students who struggle with EF difficulties feel challenged to engage in even the briefest text found in titles and subtitles. They are often accustomed to letting their eyes fly over the words, then looking to someone else and saying, "I don't get it" or "What does it mean?" The older students are so familiar with that feeling of uncertainty that they may believe that this is what happens when one reads, and that the only way to gain comprehension is to ask. Or they might ignore the task altogether. Teaching students to create an outline of the material by previewing it in this manner is like offering a road map to someone setting out on a journey. With this outline, students can then organize the details more efficiently as they read.

Highlighting $10 words in titles and subtitles gives students immediate access to the main idea of the text and the gist of the chapter in only a few minutes—usually five. (If the student doesn't own the book, a copy should be provided, either print or electronic. E-readers (Kindle, iBooks, and so on) are great for those who have access to them.) With that, the student's comprehension begins to crystallize, and the path for storage and retrieval is laid out. She becomes more able, and willing, to read the chapter for meaning and connected detail.

When students first learn to highlight, they often mark too many words or words that are interesting rather than informative. So how do you teach them to determine what's important to highlight in the paragraphs below the subtitles? We tell them to spend $10 highlighting the words that *help them understand the term(s) they marked in the subtitle above.*

Once the highlighting is complete, students are much more able to review a chapter at a glance, truly understanding the major categories and their relationships to each other. They can then use those categories to answer questions or extend their understanding in classroom activities. For those who still need more, they can type or dictate the titles and subtitles on a word processor to create a study guide and fill in the details as they read or review for tests.

Novels and Short Stories

Highlighting $10 words in novels is a little different than for textbooks—there are rarely any clear titles or subtitles to lead the way. Instead, students need to practice finding text structures that are consistent in stories. Generally speaking, structure is found in the following elements: characters and their traits, plot, theme, crisis, and resolution. As students move into the upper grades, they may also need to identify literary devices, such as flashback, foil, and metaphor. But let's begin more simply.

When reading a novel or short story, the student simply needs to highlight ($10 each) those words *that remind him what that page is about.* This may be a little basic, granted, but that's just the starting point. If a student reads a ten-page chapter, highlighting only one or two words per page, at the end of the chapter he can quickly scan back and summarize what the chapter is about. And we suggest that rather than write a summary, the student use any blank space at the back of each chapter to make two or three bullets points with short phrases that remind him what the chapter is about. Slowly, as he progresses chapter by chapter, he can look back and begin to layer the information . . . because he can *recall the information that he made decisions about* and layer that information with new higher-level concepts and opinions. Like some of the other strategies listed here, this simple "highlight and note" exercise aids working memory and long-term memory by prioritizing and organizing the important elements for students to process over time. And because all the note-taking is done in the book itself, there are no notes to organize or lose!

But what if the student doesn't own the book? Our first recommendation is to buy it, if at all possible. In some cases, of course, this is not possible because the book is a school-owned textbook or out of print, or there are financial considerations. In these cases, we recommend that the student make or receive a copy of the chapters needed and highlight those. If the student in question has a diagnosed disability that includes EF problems, perhaps this step could be part of an official accommodation. Otherwise, students should simply take chapter notes in a dedicated notebook, but this is rarely a preferred strategy because it is low in efficiency even though it is high in meaning.

If students need to track literary elements, they can add those to their highlighting protocol, highlighting quotes or scenes that jump out at them and noting them at the end of the chapter. Rather than have students add these to the small white section at the end of a chapter, however, we recommend that they create an Inspiration graphic organizer template to capture and organize their ideas.

Remember, these are scripts and routines that good readers use automatically all the time; students with EF challenges need instruction and guided practice—lots of practice—to internalize them.

Assignment Sheets

Have you ever given out a beautiful and comprehensive assignment sheet that outlines every detail of a long-term assignment, including the due dates, steps needed, sequence, materials, and smiley faces? And have you ever had a student come to you with that page within seconds and say, "I don't know what to do"?

In that little comic book bubble inside your head, you scream. Or you say things like "I didn't stay up till two in the morning making this thing just for you to say you don't get it," or "Predictable . . ."

Truth is, it *is* predictable. Lots of information given at once can be a bit overwhelming for students with EF problems. And if it's a long-term assignment, these students may already know from experience that there's a good chance they'll blow it. So what can you do?

First, ask yourself whether your assignment sheet has titles, subtitles, bullets, and check-off spaces. Next, ask yourself, does it *look* like a lot—just visually. Finally, do you need to give the whole assignment to your students at once, or can you break it down and give a little at a time? You'll hear a sigh of relief if you do.

Okay, that's for you to consider, but what do the students need to do? You may know the drill by now: they should take out their highlighter and highlight the $10 words. In other words, they will need to review the sheet piece by piece and make microdecisions about what it's saying until they have built a fuller understanding *for themselves.*

Some students will need help with this; some can do it on their own. In either case, students will usually finish reviewing the page with a greater sense of calm. Now, to keep that calm intact throughout the assignment, remember to have them enter the due date sideways in their planner and to schedule workdays!

WRITING

If reading is an input challenge, then writing needs to be considered an input *and* output challenge. In fact, writing may be one of the most complex EF tasks students face in school. It requires coming up with a thought, organizing it, putting it into words, writing or typing those words while holding the thoughts in mind over time, and tracking the whole process and all its parts. It's no wonder that students tend to freeze up at the mere thought of it! That said, writing may be one of the most important skills students can learn in school—it's the one that allows them to demonstrate their complex understandings, express themselves, state an uninterrupted opinion, and communicate over distance and time. This is the skill that gives them voice.

For many students, it is critical that we break down the writing process using warm-up strategies and organizers to help get those thoughts out.

Warm-up for Fluency: Seven-Minute Writing Samples

Recommended levels: grade 3 through adult

Two of the very important tasks of early composition include attaining automaticity and becoming comfortable with the concept of voice. Seven-minute writing samples address both of these. The process is simple: about once a week, ask students to free-write for seven minutes about anything they enjoy. Because some students don't like wide-open topics, you can offer choices too. Either way, it is important that students write about something they like or something they're good at. The only structure we impose on this activity is that

1. They write for the entire seven minutes (three to five for younger students), even if they have to make up a new topic to continue.

2. They double-space their work as a reminder that all first drafts are rough drafts with room for improvement. (This takes the pressure off too.)

3. They focus on "talking on paper" to simplify the task and encourage the use of their own writing voice.

4. They count their number of words and write that number at the top of the page near the date. You will find that with little or no prompting, students will try to beat their own last word score, thus improving their automaticity and reducing their reluctance to write. As you may have guessed, we discourage students from comparing their scores with others.

Over time, you will find that students develop a stronger and stronger sense of voice—the ten-year-olds sound like ten-year-olds, class comedians sound like comedians, deep thinkers sound deep.

Organizing: Inspiration

Recommended levels: kindergarten through adult

(We recommend Inspiration rather than Kidspiration for all levels. Because brainstorming "freestyle" can be a bit overwhelming visually, we recommend that you introduce Inspiration with the specific strategies we describe here.)

Brainstorming and organizing ideas are two additional writing skills that support both creativity and clarity of expression. These can be addressed using simple graphic organizers; however, we find that students often prefer using the computer. The software program Inspiration is perfect for this. It allows students to create their own graphic organizers as they brainstorm, and with a click of a button, it turns their brainstorm into an outline that they can rearrange as they like (see Figure 4.3). (There may be other programs that do this as well, but we are most familiar with Inspiration, and it is already in many schools.)

We like to use the "Tree" view, as most students find it less visually challenging than the "Web" view. In Figure 4.3, using a toggle, we have "hidden" the detail for Jeeps and SUVs so that this student doesn't become overwhelmed by too much detail when going to final draft (whether it's an essay or an oral presentation). We can open and close the detail as needed.

For students who develop elaborate ideas and subtopics, they can learn to "open up" only one heading at a time as they write, to keep them focused and keep their ideas tight. Although some students prefer to work in the traditional outline mode, we've found that many students prefer to organize their graphic display and write from that.

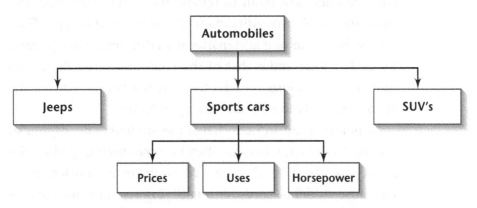

Figure 4.3   Graphic Organizer Created with Inspiration Software

Some students can get carried away with their brainstorming and end up with a page full of wildly connected, overwhelming ideas. For those students, we recommend that you create a simple template of three idea bubbles to help students constrain and focus their thoughts a bit. In our experience, students like the idea that they only need to make three major points in a paper!

Checking Your Work

Recommended levels: kindergarten through adult (once students are writing sentences)

At some point in the writing process, writers have to check their work. Although a computer can take care of some of it, there is more to be done. We recommend the following strategies.

COPS

This time-tested acronym reminds the writer to check for Capitalization, Overall sound, Punctuation, and Spelling. We ask students to write it at the top of their papers and to cross out each letter when they've finished that check. Although some students prefer to have their teachers check their rough drafts for these elements, we find that doing it themselves builds writing skills and self-reflection.

To improve students' confidence with the editing process, some teachers ask them to review their own work first and mark the number of edits made at the top of the page. Then the teacher reviews it and marks any additional edits, putting his or her total under that of the student's. Once those two numbers come close to each other, the teacher knows that the student is ready to edit more independently.

It is important to note that some students are so poor at finding their own edits that they become discouraged by the discrepancy between their own edit number and the teacher's. For those students, consider identifying two or three *kinds* of edits per assignment and let them build from that.

Learning Grammar Through Writing

If you can get your hands on an old copy, we recommend using Bell and Wheeler's *Learning Grammar Through Writing* for help with editing. This workbook is put together very differently than others we've used. It's actually a kind of guidebook of common edits, which are sorted according to categories (for example, style, punctuation, capitalization). As you go through a student's paper, you identify areas of need and use the book to find the corresponding category and item number, or code; you then write the code on the student's paper and give the student the guidebook to identify and edit the error. When the student looks up the code, she finds the grammatical rule stated and one example of how it should be used in a sentence; she then applies it to her own paper. This process of engaging personally with the rule, the example, and the application promotes the deepest kind of thinking and understanding, and therefore retention. We often find that students begin to self-correct their most common errors after editing only one paper this way.

MATH

Whereas reading and writing involve the language code, math is all about the number code. However, when it comes to executive functioning, the challenge remains centered on processing skills and cognitive strategies. In practical terms, it's about managing materials, space on the page, the sequence of math routines, and automaticity.

Math Warm-ups

Recommended levels: grade 1 through adult (once students are accurate with their math facts—addition, subtraction, multiplication or addition)

Warm-ups routines are just as important for math as they are for reading, writing, and basketball. Students warm up by timing simple skills and increasing speed, which improves automaticity. Greater automaticity frees up more room in working memory, or "RAM," to process the higher-level math concepts. There are many ways to increase automaticity of math facts and practice simple routines (such as the order of operations or the rules for adding and subtracting negative numbers), and the ones that follow are some of our favorites.

Aplusmath.com

Aplusmath.com is a free online math practice site. What we love best about this site is that students can pull up some very specific skills to practice for five to ten minutes before beginning their math work. It provides electronic flashcards that range from the basic math facts (addition, subtraction, multiplication and division) to simple algebraic clusters, negative number practice, and order of operations. Once students become familiar with the site and how to set up their warm-up time, they can begin to choose flashcard sets based on their homework that night or on an area of weakness. The site serves as a forum for building automaticity, self-reflection, and direction.

Blank Times Table

This strategy for increasing speed and automaticity was admittedly one of my (Margaret's) favorite math practices when I was in the third grade. (Some of the old ways were effective—now we know a little bit more about why!) Simply hand out blank times tables with the edges labeled 1–10 (These are readily available online.) Ask the students to complete them as fast as they can and then bring them to you to record their time. It is not unusual for this to take eight to ten minutes the first time. However, we find that these multiplication skills are not really functional unless the table can be completed in three minutes or less.

What's really interesting is to watch how students begin to speed up their times. It's not about working harder or faster; it's about working smarter. If you let them discuss their "tricks," you'll find that students begin to realize that multiplication is often nothing more than "count-bys." And almost everyone can count by ones, twos, fives, and tens. They find that the fives rows and columns are identical. They might even find the secret patterns of the nines. But what's most important is that they begin to see that math, and multiplication specifically, is often solved and encoded best by looking for patterns and strategies and by simplifying the task using "tricks" rather than just memory. These are the EF tasks that are embedded in math and the ones that deserve teachers' attention, instruction, reflection, and practice.

Triangular Flash Cards

These are simply triangular flash cards with the addends on two corners and the sum on the third, or, for multiplication, the factors on two corners and the product on the third. What makes these different is that they allow the student to cover either the addends or the sum, thus turning the practice from addition to subtraction. These cards not only afford practice for automaticity but also reinforce the fact that addition and subtraction are reverse processes—and that multiplication and division are too. Any time students can free up one part of executive functioning (working memory) at the same time that they work another (cognitive shifts), we're ecstatic!

Show All Your Work

Recommended levels: kindergarten through adult (once students begin to write math equations)

It's interesting that some teachers will read this heading and say, "Of course!" and others will say, "But they resist it so much!" or "Why?" Yet this is one of the strategies we feel more and more strongly about every year. The fact is, if students don't show their work in math, you can't be certain whether they can follow the strategies accurately and efficiently or whether they're making simple errors in calculation. If students are allowed to duplicate those mistakes day after day, they will eventually encode them in their minds as correct (remember the power of practice) and will have a harder time in the future "unraveling" those misunderstandings. If you can catch them early, you can get them on the right track.

Some teachers will accept "answers only" on homework, but require full work on tests. In this case, some students who actually understand the concepts and simple calculations may find that they lack the automaticity and speed needed to finish their tests on time. Why? Because they didn't get the eye-hand-brain practice of working those numbers out correctly and quickly during practice sets. The full task is presented only during tests. It is true that some students with EF problems also have low speed of processing, which can add to their difficulties, but we have found that some students merely lack automaticity. It's a bit tricky to sort out one from another, but because practice helps both, let it be the defining strategy.

Guided Practice

Recommended levels: kindergarten through adult

Guided practice is one of the most useful strategies for helping students with math, whether they struggle with executive functioning or with other math issues. The general idea is to meet with the student as soon as possible after a new concept has been taught. With their class work or homework in front of you, work the first problem for them, *speaking each of your thoughts out loud*. This is not repeated instruction; this is you modeling the thought process. Once you're finished, if the student is ready, have her do the next problem *speaking each though out loud* for you to monitor. If she makes an error in process, stop her and model the whole problem including that aspect of the problem for her. Continue this process until she is able to complete one or two correctly. Then have her finish the problems on her own, asking for targeted help as needed. This technique will help the student build solid routines or scripts around the new concept that should help her internalize it.

One last thought about math help: keep it positive! Even fun if you can. Research shows that math processing is often more susceptible to the effects of anxiety than other areas. Remember, anxiety and worry block information from the higher-level-thinking parts of the brain and engage the "fight or flight" areas instead. Confidence and success do the opposite!

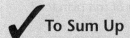

To Sum Up

- Even a carefully designed EF-Smart Classroom will not be enough for some students. At times, more individualized strategies are needed.

- Planners are the number-one tool for students who struggle with EF challenges.

- Not all students need all strategies. A careful look at their distinct problem areas will direct your choices for intervention. Table 4.1 guides this process.

- Warm-ups increase automaticity in all subject areas and reduce the EF challenges.

- Highlighting with $10 words promotes students' engagement in reading by requiring them to make a series of microdecisions about the text.

- Students with EF weaknesses require teacher guidance to learn new strategies and practice them correctly and efficiently.

? Time to Reflect

1. Choose a student. Perhaps you'll pick one who has a minor EF challenge, to see if you can create success quickly. Or perhaps you'll pick one who needs lots of help. In any case, choose a student to reflect on and consider Table 4.1. What have you already done that has worked well with this student? Does this give you any clues about how to move forward?

    _____

    _____

    _____

2. Make a plan. Pick two or three new strategies to begin with and make a plan you and the student can follow together. (See Figure 7.1, Defining a Dream Questionnaire, in Chapter Seven to begin your plan.)

    _____

    _____

    _____

3. Are there other students who might benefit from being part of this plan too?

    _____

    _____

    _____

4. Note any other key takeaways from this chapter.

    _____

    _____

    _____

The EF-Smart School

Just as small changes in the way teachers work with their whole class or individual students can facilitate the development of better executive skills, so too can administrative changes at the whole-school level support both students and teachers in these efforts.

In order to build and support executive skills throughout the grade levels, from classroom to cafeteria, and from group instruction to individual sessions, our schools may need to nudge schedules and practices a little to make room for some important strategies throughout the school day. Nothing here needs to be on a grand scale. Even minor adjustments can make room for smart conversations and strategies that help a wide range of students.

"OLD SCHOOL" TO NEW SCHOOLS

In some ways, many of our effective strategies for the classroom, the individual, and the school are nothing new—in fact they're a bit "old school" (though we write these words knowing that our "old school" of the 1960s is quite different from the "old school" of some of the educators reading this). These strategies rely on good old organization and consistency of practice, which offer students structure and predictability and therefore safe practice fields for their emerging organizational skills.

Blending a little old-school structure and practice with a little new-school process, we can apply the current Response to Intervention (RtI) approach to the whole-school level. Let's look at how James Hale describes RtI and its roots in good instructional practice:

> The basic ideas of RtI were developed over a century ago in the behavioral tradition of psychology. These ideas are relatively simple. You collect data over time and adjust instruction until the child achieves success.
>
> A teacher modifies instruction (intervention) to help a struggling child, and then checks the child's progress regularly (called progress monitoring) to see if the intervention is working. If the intervention is working, the problem is solved. If the intervention is not working, you change the intervention and monitor progress. This process continues until the child improves. This approach does not rely on diagnosing the child, but focuses on whether the child has a "skill deficit" or a "performance deficit," and provides help until the child gets better.[1]

This RtI model offers a framework for looking at the larger student body, and it has been a hot topic on the educational circuit in recent years. A visual model helps us to consider the levels of support likely to be needed by the students in any given school (see Figure 5.1). Although we include percentages as a guide, these will certainly vary a bit from school to school. If your school's actual student need for EF intervention is not yet clear, you may like to begin with our percentages and modify them as needed.

If we apply the RtI model to our consideration of students with weak executive skills, we can expect the general supports in an EF-Smart Classroom (see Chapter Three) to be effective for approximately 80 percent of our population. That's a pretty effective level of support!

With those general supports in place, perhaps another 20 percent will show need for additional help. We can design

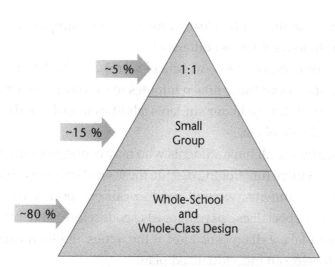

Figure 5.1 Schoolwide Response to Intervention

some small-group approaches by starting with the strategies from the EF-Smart Classroom. However, for this small group, we apply the strategies with greater frequency than we do with the whole class. These students also need more opportunities for self-reflection. If we add more targeted interventions from Chapter Four, then we have an intervention plan that can be quite effective. However, educators will need a time and a place during the day when this work can be done efficiently and discreetly.

In some schools, small groups meet in a section of the library or resource center for fifteen minutes at the beginning or end of the day. Instruction in executive routines does not require a long teaching period. Rather, it seems to be most effective when the content is the student's actual schoolwork, schedules, and expectations, and the sessions are relatively brief. Fifteen minutes is all it takes, although the frequency may vary from two to five times per week, depending on the student.

With a quiet and supportive start or end to the day, students are able to successfully apply and generalize the skills they're working on. As we've said in earlier chapters, it's the teacher's ability to be clear, consistent, and supportive that seems to make the most difference.

It's our responsibility as school teams and leaders to find those places and those fifteen minutes in the day if we want to truly effect change in our students' abilities to make and carry out academic plans.

Finally, we all have students who may continue to struggle with executive functioning despite these levels of intervention. For those students, we will need to call on specialized help (learning specialists, psychologists, counselors, and others) who can take a diagnostic look at the issues and their causes, and develop an individualized plan.

Let's go back to our biking metaphor. Just as we don't assume that everyone will learn to ride at the same time or with the same degree of skill, neither do we expect all of them to be up to the same level of challenge. (Whereas some struggle to manage a simple flat course, others are up to riding ramps, trail riding, or even racing the Tour de France!) Clearly, it is the job of school administrators to look at the course set out for the whole student body and to be certain that the levels of challenge make sense for most students while also providing additional support for those who need more help.

If teachers and administrators together can structure the degree of challenge correctly for our population of students, students will progress to higher levels of executive functioning with the fewest bumps and bruises, and achieve the most success. In order to lay the course well in each school, administrators will need to utilize the professional insights and skills of all of their educators and provide them with the tools and feedback they require to carry this out.

How do we do this? By using the tools we have available to us: scheduling, carefully allocating our scarce resources, and finding times when educators can communicate and plan together.

FACULTY MEETINGS

If your school already has dedicated times for faculty and team meetings, then hooray—your work is half done! If not, you will need to create regular and consistent meeting times in order to examine and solve the challenges of executive functioning throughout your school.

The Effective Faculty Meeting

Within the effective faculty meeting, addressing issues of executive functioning simply means putting them on the agenda, perhaps using protocols for discussion, then examining and planning for student success. Items for discussion might include

1. What are the executive skill demands in your school?

2. What supports do you already have in place? Which work and which do not?

3. Is there an area of need you can address together?

   a. Will it require reallocating time? Personnel? Volunteers?

   b. Will you need a team to examine this further?

Using Protocols

If you don't already have a dynamic format for discussing these kinds of topics within faculty meetings, consider using protocols to gain clarity and action on important topics in as little as forty-five minutes. Protocols are structured conversations that organize interactions in groups and lead to smart and productive meetings. *The Power of Protocols: An Educator's Guide to Better Practice*[2] and *The Right Question Institute* (www .rightquestion.org) are two great resources for protocols.

If you have school teams that would like to enhance their leadership skills while developing new action plans, consider the online course Leading for Understanding, by Project Zero at Harvard University. Not only can you share your challenges and solutions with others in the country, but you'll get to compare notes with educators around the world! We'll use a version of Project Zero's Action Plan in Chapter Seven.

GATHERING REFERENCES

In order to allow faculty to dig deeper into EF topics as needs arise, it is important to gather references and make them easily accessible. In addition, providing RSS feeds will allow them opportunities for ongoing professional development. We have listed some of our favorite books and websites here.

Books

Gathering a few essential, up-to-date books is important for any faculty. We currently recommend the following:

Late, Lost, and Unprepared, by Joyce Cooper-Kahn and Laurie Dietzel (Bethesda, MD: Woodbine House, 2008)

> This book about executive functioning was written for parents, but provides good information for teachers as well. It gives an overview of executive functioning as well as specific recommendations for interventions.

Brain Rules: 12 Principles for Surviving and Thriving at Work, Home, and School, by John Medina (Seattle: Pear Press, 2008)

> This author writes in an engaging and humorous style, summarizing research relevant to how people learn and perform in school and elsewhere. The book comes with a DVD that is surprisingly entertaining as well as informative.

Challenged Kids, Challenged Teachers: Teaching Students with Tourette's, Bipolar Disorder, Executive Dysfunction, OCD, ADHD, and More, by Leslie E. Packer and Sheryl K. Pruitt (Bethesda, MD: Woodbine House, 2010)

> This practical book discusses the educational impact of some of the more complex disorders that usually include deficits in executive functioning.

The Executive Brain: Frontal Lobes and the Civilized Mind, by Elkhonon Goldberg (New York: Oxford University Press, 2001)

> This book is for those who are eager to dig into the subject of how the brain functions and the role of executive functioning in our lives.

Websites

Keeping links of important websites is an important tool for remaining current on EF issues. As of this writing, we like the following:

Edutopia:http://www.edutopia.org/blog/improving-executive-function-judy-willis-md

> Judy Willis is a researcher and educator whose work we trust and enjoy.

National Center for Learning Disabilities: http://www.ncld .org/ld-basics/ld-aamp-executive-functioning/basic-ef-facts/ what-is-executive-function

> This site offers a simple overview of executive functioning that is particularly helpful to parents and teachers who are new to the discussion.

LDOnline: http://www.ldonline.org/

> This website is both professional and current and offers a concise view of executive functioning along with other learning problems. It provides advice for parents and teachers alike.

THE MAGIC FORMULA

There is none. Although we'd like to be able to say that there is a magic formula for addressing executive functioning in schools, just like every other problem we face in our schools, it really comes down to a few simple moves: increasing our understanding of executive functioning, examining our population, examining the challenges and resources in our own school, and working through a series of collaborative and dynamic conversations dedicated to solving those challenges.

Remember, the faculty and staff involved in these conversations and eventual interventions will have their own varied levels of executive functioning. Your full faculty may need a humorous and candid conversation about these issues too in order to plan well together. It can be fascinating, as long as it stays respectful!

As administrators begin to look for signs of EF skills in their faculty, consider also the effect of pairing students and teachers who have low EF skills. If the teacher designs learning tasks and assessments that are low in organization, his or her students with low executive skills will struggle dramatically and often fail. It is important to consider either training those teachers in organizational techniques (for both materials and concept development), pairing them with others with stronger skills, or placing struggling students in another class. Ideally, all teachers should be able to accommodate students with low executive skills in their classes, but some may need time to learn the skills themselves first.

We realize that there may be some schools out there that have gone through this process and have more to offer all of us. We'd love to hear from you, and we'd love to find a way to share with each other. They say a topic is never complete when a book goes to print; it's just "ready enough." Perhaps we'll meet again to discuss this topic some way . . . in print or in person.

✔ **To Sum Up**

- School administrators and teachers need to work together to implement effective schoolwide change to create EF-Smart Schools.

- Response to Intervention provides a model for fine-tuning school structure and allocating resources.

- School administrators need to oversee the EF challenges throughout the school to ensure smooth progress in students over time.

- Effective, efficient faculty meetings are essential for identifying and changing EF practices. There are specific protocols designed for educational settings that can structure and focus those meetings.

- Online and print resources help anchor faculty members in current thinking and pedagogy.

? Time to Reflect

1. What aspects of your current school design are most effective for sup-porting the development of executive functioning? (Consider schedul-ing, routines, personnel, meeting times.) Which areas can be changed to provide the most impact?

    _____

    _____

    _____

2. What areas of instruction are most effective in your school for supporting exec-utive functioning? Which areas could be changed to provide greater impact? Remember, the targets for intervention could be different at every school—do you need to address EF skills for the entire student body, or will you achieve the greatest impact by addressing students with severe skill deficits? Consider using the Question Formulation Technique protocol from the Right Question Institute (www.rightquestion.org) with your faculty if you need help defining your school's unique challenges.

    _____

    _____

    _____

3. What literature and websites are currently available to faculty? Which materials would you like to add, and how will you make them available?

    _____

    _____

    _____

4. Note any other key takeaways from this chapter.

    _____

    _____

    _____

How the Specialist Can Help

6

Although as we've noted, most students with EF problems can succeed in the classroom with teacher interventions and modifications, some will need a more specialized approach. So we need not only to examine the EF-Smart Classroom and the EF-sensitive student but also, when we get to the top of the RtI pyramid, to examine ways to tailor or intensify an individual student plan.

What models will help you understand a student's more intensive instructional needs? Which tools can you use to address those that are the most complex? The complexity of a student's needs is likely to be a function of mixed variables, such as attention deficits combined with acute anxiety. Or diabetes combined with missed instruction. Or chronic depression with learning disabilities. With this level of complexity, you often need something more.

At this point, for you to maximize the impact and support for the student, you need to intensify your diagnostic-remediation approach by bringing in learning specialists. In this chapter, we will look at specific ways to examine the learning task in relation to the individual student, how to facilitate greater independence, and how to consult with teachers and other professionals in order to generalize those skills in a busy classroom environment.

EXAMINING THE LEARNING TASK AND ITS EF DEMANDS

Picture this: student in one hand, assignment in the other. Consider the executive demands of the assignment; consider the EF skills of the student—how do you get these to mesh?

First, let's consider the student. Good executive functioning involves a chain of events. In the EF-Smart Classroom, we try to build these sequences proactively. When students have trouble performing despite these efforts, then we need to figure out where in the chain of events the student is getting stuck. Targeted intervention is always aimed at the point of failure—moving forward from the last successful behavior in the chain and building the steps toward the goal one at a time.

Second, we consider the assignment. There are many models available for examining classroom instruction, materials, and assessments—but for our purposes, we have chosen to use Bloom's Revised Taxonomy because it allows us to specify the nature of the task we present to the student.[1] Do we intend to build and assess knowledge of history? Are we teaching to develop deeper understanding of a process in science? Or are we asking the student to analyze, synthesize, and create a new application in math? Each of these requires different internal organizers and processes that we sometimes take for granted. Using the revised taxonomy, we can clarify these structures and tailor them to the specific skill sets of a specific student who struggles.

The supports we discuss in this section are aimed at organizing students' thoughts by making them more visible, bringing those thoughts consciously to a new level or organization, and then enabling students to reinternalize them to create greater efficiency. To do this we rely heavily on some templates from Inspiration and some apps for iPad. However, if these are not available, equivalent graphic organizers have always worked well.

We will begin our discussion here by considering two broad categories: lower-order thinking (more concrete), and higher-order thinking (more abstract). To understand these most deeply, you might like to choose a particular assignment to analyze. First, determine which kinds of thinking it taps into and consider its recommended organizer or app. Then, by overlaying the thinking demands of the assignment onto the matching graphic organizer, you create a visual representation of each thinking process.

Although we have chosen certain templates and apps to share with you, it is important to remember that these are just samples of the kinds of graphic organizers that can help make student thinking visible—there are certainly others. We thank Julia Maxey, educational technologist, for compiling and sorting the iPad apps listed in the next sections. If you are like us, you may want to rely on a technology specialist in your school or district to help you with your first "electronic intervention."

We realize that in a very short period of time, these templates and apps will become outdated and may be replaced by new ones. Our intention is to introduce you to a variety of graphic organizers with which you can become familiar and that can support your important EF work.

We will keep the following outline of thinking skills intentionally brief for easy application, and then finish with a few thoughts about how to help students internalize their new-found executive skills.

Lower-Order Thinking

The lower-order thinking skills in Bloom's Revised Taxonomy include *remembering* and *understanding*. These are defined here with a brief focusing question, some signal verbs that indicate when they're in use, and some examples of organizers and apps that structure and support each skill's executive features.

Remembering: Can the student recall or remember the information?

Sample directions: Name the bones in the hand.

Signal verbs: define, duplicate, list, memorize, name, recall, repeat, reproduce, state

Inspiration templates: Concept Map, Science Vocabulary List, Tree Diagram

Apps: Evernote, Sundry Notes, Dropbox, Safari, Penultimate, FlashCards

Note: It is important to note that even though we include flash card apps that support rote memorization, we recommend that they be grouped by similar features or concepts to further strengthen both memory and understanding. Concept Maps and Tree Diagrams do this grouping more automatically.

Understanding: Can the student explain ideas or concepts?

Sample directions: Explain the importance of the Bill of Rights at the time it was passed.

Signal verbs: classify, describe, discuss, explain, paraphrase, recognize, report, translate

Inspiration templates: KWL (Know, Wonder, Learn) Organizer, Classification

Apps: Google Docs, Pages, iTunes U, 123 Charts, Simplemind

Note: It is clear from the kinds of organizers listed in this section that we are truly digging into the ability to organize concepts into categories. These concepts can be very concrete (for example, groups of vegetables or modes of transportation), or they can be more abstract (such as forms of government or philosophies of education). In either case, these organizers offer a structure that helps students grasp the information and that serves as a template that can be internalized over time.

Higher-Order Thinking

The higher-order thinking skills in Bloom's Revised Taxonomy include *applying, analyzing, evaluating,* and *creating*. We follow the same format here as for the lower-order thinking skills.

Applying: Can the student use the information in a new way?

> **Sample directions:** Illustrate what you think might happen next in the story.
>
> **Signal verbs:** choose, demonstrate, dramatize, employ, illustrate, interpret, operate, schedule, sketch, solve, use, write
>
> **Inspiration templates:** Decision Tree, Problem Solving Process
>
> **Apps:** Educreations (whiteboard app), 123 Charts, Google Earth, ShareBoard, ArtRage

Note: Applying requires a base level of understanding that has to be maintained while working memory searches for new ways of applying that understanding. This level of thinking requires a lot from working memory; these organizers are needed to create a concrete way to hold on to information and work with it at the same time. As is the case with many other levels of understanding, students with EF problems may be intelligent enough to work with these parts, just not efficient enough to manipulate them internally . . . yet.

Analyzing: Can the student distinguish between the different parts?

Sample directions: Compare the use of light in these two paintings.

Signal verbs: appraise, compare, contrast, criticize, differentiate, discriminate, distinguish, examine, experiment, question, test

Inspiration templates: Compare and Contrast, Cause and Effect, Root Cause Analysis

Apps: iThoughtsHD, MagicalPad, Numbers, 123 Charts, Popplet

Note: With analyzing, we are asking students to have strong knowledge and understanding of one or more concepts and also to understand the abstract structures that define them or differentiate them from each other. As with applying, the acts of "holding" and "manipulating" information become the executive challenges here, and these organizers provide a kind of external storage.

Evaluating: Can the student justify a stand or decision?

Sample directions: Evaluate our song selection and placement for the play.

Signal verbs: appraise, argue, defend, evaluate, judge, select, support, value

Inspiration templates: Website Credibility, Impact Innovation

Apps: Numbers, Good Reads, Flipboard

Note: Evaluating requires the student to maintain knowledge within a broader understanding, understand the concept's defining features, and make decisions about its appropriateness in novel situations.

Does it begin to feel as though we're trying to juggle more and more balls? It certainly does to some students, but these templates should help.

Creating: Can the student create a new product or point of view?

Sample directions: Design an environmentally green solution to the water flow problem.

Signal verbs: assemble, construct, create, design, develop, formulate, write

Inspiration templates: Opinion Support, Project Plan

Apps: Voicethread, iMovie, Garageband, iPhoto, camera functions, Keynote, Comic Life, Animoto, Prezi, Google Earth, Penultimate, Wordcloud, ShareBoard, ArtRage

Note: Suffice it to say that in creating, the student needs all of the other levels of thinking to some degree, plus the ability to express his new understanding successfully in a tangible way. When creating, the student is rapidly cycling through input and output with lots of processing in between. These templates help capture students' thoughts in the midst of cycling and allow them to put their energy into manipulating the information rather than just trying to keep track of it. So the templates allow students not only to achieve new levels of organization but also to develop enough clarity to be able to demonstrate their understanding to others. At this level, the new product or performance becomes public, and students want their skills to be at their very best.

The assignments that you might choose to examine in light of the Bloom's Revised Taxonomy levels we've outlined here will probably address more than one mode of thinking, so you may need more than one organizer, or a hybrid, to support the student with EF problems. The decision about what organizer to use may seem daunting at first, but when you attack assignments one at a time, the picture becomes much clearer. In fact, the clarity this decision brings will usually help you design your next assignment with a more precise understanding of the EF skills embedded in each task.

One of the most interesting benefits of using these organizers over time is that they help students internalize the executive template needed. If you are careful to introduce only one or two at a time and give the student enough practice with each, she will begin to know when and how to employ each one. As we mentioned in Chapter Four, we know a student who reached a fluid level with Inspiration and eventually was able to open up a particular organizer independently . . . in his head! Once he visualized the template, he was able to describe the three major parts, add new information to it, and come out with a clearly organized response to a complex question— something he had never done before!

EXAMINING EF SKILLS FOR LEVELS OF AUTOMATICITY AND INDEPENDENCE: The Four-Quadrant Model

As mentioned in earlier chapters, there are ways of identifying the specific EF challenges for each student. These include examining classroom performance; considering teacher, student, and parent input; and factoring in the results from formal checklists and standardized testing. The RtI approach outlined in Chapter Five suggests that we need to become more and more comprehensive in our interventions in response to a student's ability to perform independently. How do we know the difference between a student who is not making progress and one who is experiencing the normal wobbliness that occurs when we take off the training wheels? When a student has struggled with the same issue over a long period of time, it is time to shift the focus to a progression of strategies that is specifically designed to build independence.

Helping students succeed with executive functioning requires building both skills and independence, and unfortunately our approach to building independence can often be a "hit or miss" effort.

Borrowing from an approach that grew out of cognitive psychology and has been implemented by occupational therapists in Australia, we will use the Four-Quadrant Model of Facilitated Learning (4QM), which can help us plan for building independence more consciously.[2] We describe the elements of our adaptation of the 4QM in the next sections.

If you are a visual processor, you might like to use the diagram (Figure 6.1) for an initial assessment of independent performance or as a map to plan for future levels of support. If you are more of a text person, you can similarly use our written descriptions to assess and plan. Either way, you may find it useful to export your thinking about levels of independent functioning onto the planning template in Chapter Seven (Figure 7.2) if you need to develop a specific plan for a student.

The 4QM serves as a scaffold for understanding, planning, and coordinating the use of learning strategies. The researchers explain:

> The 4QM groups together the various cognitive and physical learning strategies useful in leading clients to perform . . . tasks more autonomously, based on differing learner needs. Two continua—directness of approach and source of initiation—are integrated to define four distinct clusters of learning strategies, each serving specific learner needs.

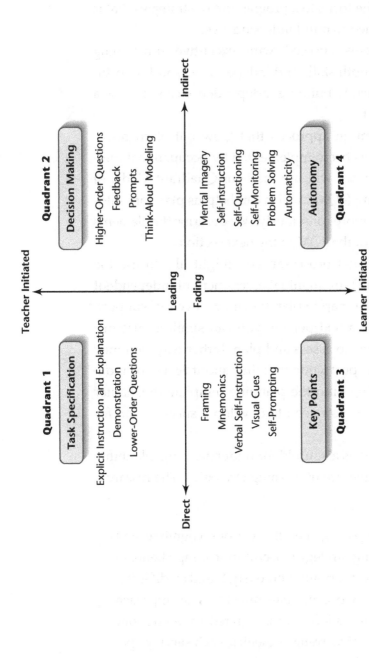

Figure 6.1 The Four-Quadrant Model of Facilitated Learning

Source: Adapted with permission from Greber, C., Ziviani, J., and Rodger, S. "The Four-Quadrant Model of Facilitated Learning (Part 2): Strategies and Applications," *Australian Occupational Therapy Journal,* 2007, 54(Suppl. 1), S41.

Those strategies that are direct and initiated by a facilitator (Quadrant 1) specify the characteristics of the task and/or the performance required. Other strategies that are indirect in nature, yet still facilitator-initiated, fall into Quadrant 2. These are useful in encouraging decision-making by the learner. Quadrant 3 groups those overt self-prompting strategies initiated by the learner that help the learner to recall key points essential to task performance. Autonomous performance is underpinned by a range of self-regulatory strategies that are not obvious to observers and these strategies are grouped in Quadrant 4. The 4QM helps therapists to coordinate the learning strategies used to promote autonomy by selecting strategies that meet the changing needs of the learner as skill acquisition proceeds.[3]

Quadrant 1—Direct Facilitator-Initiated Strategies

Quadrant 1 includes task-specific, highly directive strategies that may be essential for initially engaging a student who has experienced failure with one or more EF tasks. These strategies include explicit instruction and explanation, demonstration, guided practice, and lower-order questioning (about knowledge and understanding).

An example of a Quadrant 1 activity might include instruction in planner use. If the student has a planner but doesn't seem to know how to fill it in properly, direct instruction or demonstration may be needed to get her on the road to independence. Or perhaps the student has been instructed and can explain exactly how to do it, but does not carry it out independently. In this case, she may need intensive guided practice to find success and build independence.

Again, success is our first goal, but independent success is our ultimate aim. Once guided practice is successful, we can move to Quadrant 2 strategies to further promote independence.

Quadrant 2—Indirect Facilitator-Initiated Strategies

The strategies in Quadrant 2 are more indirect decision-making strategies designed to bring students to the next level of independence. These strategies include higher-order questioning (about application, analysis, evaluation, and creation), feedback, prompts, and think-aloud modeling. Greber, Ziviani, and Rodger note, "When the learner understands the task requirements, but is unable to generate an effective plan for performing the task, different learning tools are necessary. Strategies that engage the learner in decision-making have different features to those that specify the task. Although they remain facilitator-initiated, they are less direct in nature. These strategies aim to engage the learner in the decision-making process and are represented in Quadrant 2."[4]

Using our planner example, the strategies might include asking the middle school student, "What will you need to do with your planner, now that you have the assignment sheet and have underlined the major sections?" Or perhaps the high school student, "Now that you have your partner for the project, what will be your next step?" Though these may sound like simple moves, students with EF problems may need our external prompts to consider the next step in a series.

Once students master these Quadrant 2 skills, they are ready to go on to a more self-regulated approach.

Quadrant 3—Direct Learner-Initiated Strategies

Continuing to work within the model of increasing independence, Quadrant 3 helps orient the student toward self-questioning about key points of a task. At this level of independence, prompting turns into priming (strategies that rehearse learned procedures to ensure that the intended response is the correct one). Additional strategies include mnemonics, verbal self-instruction, and visual cues.

To address transitioning in performance from "other-regulation" to "self-regulation," Greber and colleagues state, "Early forms of self-regulation include learner-initiated self-prompting to focus on the key features of performance. These features might be procedural (such as the steps of the task), outcome-focused (the goal of the task), or strategy-based prompts (tactics related to the performance)."[5]

If a student were studying for a test with the increased independence defined by this quadrant, he might recognize the need to turn a long list into a mnemonic device to help him retain the information. Or to create a visual reminder to do something later, the student might choose to put a rubber band around his wrist.

Quadrant 4—Indirect Learner-Initiated Strategies

"When learners do not exhibit signs of self-prompting during successful performance, they can be considered to be functioning in Quadrant 4."[6]

This final level of independence includes such strategies as mental imagery, self-instruction, self-questioning, self-monitoring, problem solving, and automaticity. It is probably safe to say that a student operating at this level of executive functioning would not be considered to have an EF problem at all.

However, it is important to remember that executive skills do not come as a package deal. Students who achieve independent success in one area may still need help with other aspects of executive functioning. This is where you need to apply careful analysis, skill, and monitoring to determine the next essential area to be addressed in the student plan.

And in order to be truly successful, students must be able to generalize their increasingly independent executive skills to different assignments, different teachers, and varying workloads. When our students are ready to move out of direct, one-on-one services, our role as specialist shifts to that of consultant.

CONSULTING WITH TEACHERS

Why do some students have success in the resource center or counseling office, but fail to generalize it to their broader classroom experiences? As specialists working individually with students, we clarify the learning task and assess student skills and levels of independence. Now it becomes our job to "set the stage" for the student in the regular classroom.

Fortunately, the tools needed to do this successfully for our students are probably familiar to you: co-planning, co-teaching, and reassessing and planning as a team.

Co-Planning

When planning for a student who struggles with executive functioning, we want to be sure that team members are asking targeted questions.

1. Has someone carefully analyzed the lesson and assignments for Bloom's Revised Taxonomy levels and the organizers needed to support it?

2. Is someone bringing a clear understanding of the student's specific executive skills to the discussion table?

3. Is it clear what level of independence the student brings to the task in question?

With these questions clearly addressed, co-planners can confidently design an intervention that is well targeted and that brings the strongest opportunities for success. If no one has taken on the role of asking and answering these questions yet, then who might be in a position to begin this process?

Co-Teaching

Co-teaching requires the same clarity about the student, the task, and the level of independence as co-planning does; however, it may have a more fluid feel. Using the guided questions for co-planning, the in-class specialist will be able to assess and intervene continuously, also evaluating issues that may impact executive learning and performance, such as the student's level of stress or fatigue.

Rather than focus on a student's level of reading, writing, or math skills as many specialists do, the specialist concerned with executive functioning needs to monitor the student's ability to organize, initiate, and self-monitor as she moves through a series of classroom routines. And the specialist needs to monitor with an eye to increasing independence.

Reassessing and Planning Together

Classroom instructional demands change constantly—and so do our students, as they learn and practice and as they mature neurologically. Our ability to cycle through the process of co-planning and co-teaching as we continuously monitor and plan for that change is what will determine the long-term success for the student with EF problems. And it is our ability to rely on each other as a team that will keep that task manageable.

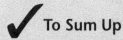

To Sum Up

- When a student has more severe problems with executive functioning, a specialist may be needed to examine the student's skills in light of current academic demands.

- Bloom's Taxonomy can be used to clarify the complexity of certain assignments and allows educators to carefully choose graphic organizers and apps that will help support a student's efforts to meet the EF demands of the task.

- Graphic organizers and apps are helpful because these tools capture students' thoughts in a visible and concrete manner while the students continue to manipulate the information.

- Effective remediation relies on the specialist's ability to understand a student's levels of automaticity and independence with EF demands. A simple visual using a four-quadrant model can help the specialist clarify these levels.

- In order to effectively generalize the EF successes of a student from an individual or small-group setting to the larger classroom, co-planning with teachers is essential.

? **Time to Reflect**

1. How do you already promote independent learning and performance in your students?

   _____

   _____

   _____

2. Focusing on one student, can you chart his approximate place in the 4QM? What new level can you visualize in the next month? Are there other students who could possibly move to that level too?

   _____

   _____

   _____

3. In what ways do you co-plan or co-teach? Are there ways to include these approaches in your plans to move your students toward independence?

   _____

   _____

   _____

4. Note any other key takeaways from this chapter.

   _____

   _____

   _____

Planning for Change

7

Just as students work in a complex world of swirling concepts and routines and expectations, so too do teachers. We deal constantly with classroom expectations, school requirements, and district goals. When we add the complexity of helping students with different learning styles, the demands can become overwhelming at times.

Frustration, anxiety, tension. Richard Lavoie identifies these as attributes that get in the way of student learning and performance.[1] But as educators, aren't we learners and performers too? Aren't we susceptible to the same interferences as our students? And although a book like this may relieve some educators because it offers insight and strategies they're looking for, other educators will feel the stress of needing to do even more with too little time and insufficient resources. So how can you begin to make changes in your classroom or school without creating more stress?

You can begin to make gentle changes by doing for yourself what you do for your students: assess, plan and organize, act, and reassess. You assess the greatest areas of need in your classrooms, practices, students, or schools. You plan and organize your resources in *one specific* area. You act and repeat, act and repeat until you see progress. And you reassess intermittently to again pinpoint the greatest area of need. You cannot do it all at once. As we promised in the beginning and then again throughout the book, we'll look at a simple model of action and reflection that is meant to be applicable in the tiny slivers of time we all have for planning.

Throughout Part Two, we have looked at ways of examining executive skills in terms of the individual, the assignment, the classroom, and the school. We have offered suggestions to help clarify, accommodate, and intervene. In this chapter, these concepts and concerns become yours to plan for. Just as with your students, you cannot plan to change everything at once. You must choose carefully and assess just which element is most important to address today. Is it a severe individual concern that needs attention? Is there a pattern of problems that impact a range of students? Or is there a conversation that needs to take place to bring your whole school into agreement on how to address executive functioning and its challenges?

Each school is different. Each time of the year and each grade level presents its own challenges. So what is your challenge area? What do you need to plan to change?

The first section of this chapter will help you isolate these important questions using the Defining a Dream Questionnaire. The second section introduces you to the Planning and Reflection Guide. The third takes you through the planning process, using case examples with dramatically different problems of practice that demonstrate how one might use both the questionnaire and the guide to address different EF issues. In the end, however, the materials in this chapter are yours—yours to use as you see fit, whether you are acting as an individual, a small team, or a large group examining the question of executive functioning in your school.

DEFINING A PROBLEM OF PRACTICE

Before we jump into planning to improve executive functioning in your classroom, it is important to pause and reflect on the issue(s) you or your team would like to address. In order to identify issues that go deep into the learning process or that broadly affect the learning environment, you need to build a dream or topic that is truly generative (capable of originating and producing new solutions and direction). Our list of generative questions in Figure 7.1, the Defining a Dream Questionnaire, will help you expand your EF dreams so that they are not only clear and effective but also powerful, meaningful, and broad enough to create the greatest impact.

In order to create a generative dream or goal, you must first describe a problem of practice as it pertains to an individual or a group of students. Next, consider some follow-up questions to help you become more specific and concrete about your goals. The Defining a Dream Questionnaire (Figure 7.1) takes you through this process.

PLANNING AND REFLECTION GUIDE

Once your generative dream has become clear using the questionnaire, you can begin to plan for change. Figure 7.2, the Planning and Reflection Guide, asks you to write down your dream or goal clearly. You will also need to assess where the student(s) or school (or both) stands in terms of that goal. Next, you will name the mysteries that keep you from knowing clearly how to act to reach your dream. Finally, you will plan to act, and those actions should be designed to both eliminate your mysteries and achieve your dreams. (In the next section, we'll look at several examples of how the template and guide might be used.) Action plans are works in progress, so you will need to revisit them from time to time when your dreams are realized or new problems arise. Figure 7.3 illustrates these continuous cycles of action and reflection. It's important to note that although we have presented this process in a certain order using the planning guide, you can begin anywhere in the cycle that makes sense to you and your problem of practice. Just be certain to complete the cycle for the greatest impact!

Figure 7.1   Defining a Dream Questionnaire

Describe your problem of practice:

_____

_____

_____

_____

1. Why is this issue of central importance to you, your student, your practice, or your school? What are its essential features?

    _____

    _____

    _____

    _____

2. What are its greatest areas of impact? What else does it impact?

    _____

    _____

    _____

    _____

3. How has it been addressed so far, and why does it need to be addressed differently now?

    _____

    _____

    _____

    _____

4. Who may be able to help formulate a new plan?

    _____

    _____

    _____

    Using your responses to the preceding questions, summarize your problem of practice as a more generative dream. If it helps, highlight the $10 words from each of your four responses and use them in your description.

    _____

    _____

    _____

    _____

Figure 7.2 Planning and Reflection Guide

Name or Topic:	Area(s) of Need:	Date
Assessment What do you already know about your student, class(es), program(s), or school(s)? Use observation notes, BRIEFs, formal and informal assessments.		
Dream Define the dream you will aim for (use the generative dream you created in the Defining a Dream Questionnaire). Are there other issues that can be addressed by that same dream?		
Mysteries What do you still need to know in order to act? Are there any assumptions that need to be challenged? Are there resources you need? Are there people, protocols, or permissions you need to gather?		
Actions What actions can you take to eliminate the mysteries and attain your dreams?		
Evidence What specific evidence will indicate that you have closed the gap or reached your goal? Make your "evidence" as specific and observable as possible. Pose a question to reassess more broadly and begin the cycle again if needed.		

Source: Adapted from Wilson, D., Perkins, D., Bonnet, D., Miani, C., and Unger, C. *Learning at Work.* Cambridge, MA: Project Zero, 2005; and the WIDE World online professional development course Leading for Understanding 1 Action Project Guide.

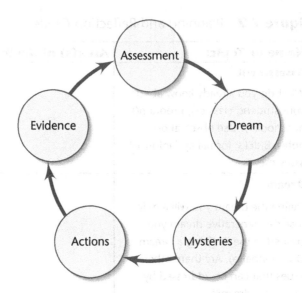

Figure 7.3 Cycles of Action and Reflection

USING THE TEMPLATE AND GUIDE: CASE EXAMPLES

To demonstrate how you might use the Defining a Dream Questionnaire and the Planning and Reflection Guide, we will look at the following cases:

Case 1—four students in a third-grade class are never ready to begin class on time.

Case 2—a fifteen-year old girl has trouble finishing her homework and turning things in.

Case 3—reading is discovered to be a fluency and EF problem for students in multiple grade levels.

Please note that in the sample Defining a Dream Questionnaires, the highlighting of $10 words is indicated by *bold italics*.

Case 1—Third-Grade Class: Beginning on Time

The text of the Case 1 Defining a Dream Questionnaire follows.

Describe your problem of practice:

It is the end of the first quarter, and I still have *four students* who don't seem to know how to *begin* the school day well. One stands and talks at the door, two wander around from their cubbies to the work stations and never make it to circle time without my direct intervention, and one always seems to drop the homework folder somewhere other than his desk. How can I get them to get to our first activity like everyone else?

1. Why is this issue of central importance to you, your student, your practice, or your school? What are its essential features?

    I am concerned that they are forming really **bad habits**. While some of these students have problems with organization and following directions throughout the day, their problems at beginning of the day seem to get us all off on the wrong foot.

2. What are its greatest areas of impact? What else does it impact?

    Their poor start to the day not only gets them off on the wrong foot but ends up *stealing instructional time* from the other students who are ready to learn.

3. How has it been addressed so far, and why does it need to be addressed differently now?

    I have reminded them over and over again and led each one of them through the steps personally. The problem is, while I help one of them, the other three are wandering around. It's like trying to herd cats! At this point one of the students is *beginning to push back*.

4. Who may be able to help formulate a new plan?

I'm not sure, but *another pair of hands* might help.

Using your responses to the preceding questions, summarize your problem of practice as a more generative dream. If it helps, highlight the $10 words from each of your four responses and use them in your description.

Table 7.1 Case 1 Planning and Reflection Guide

Name or Topic:	Area(s) of Need:	Date
Four students in the morning	*Four students have trouble beginning the day well*	*10/20*
Assessment What do you already know about your student, class(es), program(s), or school(s)? Use observation notes, BRIEFs, formal and informal assessments.	*One of the students is diagnosed with ADHD, two are best friends, and one just seems to have a lot to say in the morning. I have been concerned about the one who is being so social, as it continues throughout the day.*	*10/20*
Dream Define the dream you will aim for (use the generative dream you created in the Defining a Dream Questionnaire). Are there other issues that can be addressed by that same dream?	*I would like four of my students to begin the instructional day smoothly, forming good habits and contributing to the group instructional time.*	*10/20*
Mysteries What do you still need to know in order to act? Are there any assumptions that need to be challenged? Are there resources you need? Are there people, protocols, or permissions you need to gather?	*Have there been any changes in the student with ADHD lately—growth, family changes, etc?*	*10/20*

Table 7.1 Case 1 Planning and Reflection Guide (*Continued*)

Name or Topic:	Area(s) of Need:	Date
Actions What actions can you take to eliminate the mysteries and attain your dreams?	*Check with the special educator about the ADHD issue.* *Contact parents of others to check on the mysteries above. Also let them know that I will be starting a new plan soon about how to begin the day. More on that later...* *Ask another faculty member to observe the start of the day to see if there is anything else to consider.* *The student with ADHD has had a growth spurt lately, and the parents will check with their doctor to see if the medication is correct. They were concerned too lately.* *The students who are friends have always been that way...*	*10/20*
	The talkative student has recently had a new little brother. Mom will have her aunt spend more time with her. Our academic coach sees the same things I do. We will work together to • *Talk to the four students as a group* • *Walk them through the routine with no one else in the room* • *Ask them to walk though the routine together, identifying each step* • *Walk through the routine with the whole group and the academic coach monitoring* *If that is not enough, we will set up a positive reinforcement chart for those who need it.*	*10/25*
	Two of the students will need a chart to succeed.	*11/2*
Evidence What specific evidence will indicate that you have closed the gap or reached your goal? Make your "evidence" as specific and observable as possible.	*The students will independently* 1. *Hang up their coats* 2. *Go straight to their cubbies with backpacks and work.* 3. *Go straight to circle time and have a seat.*	*10/20*
Pose a question to reassess more broadly and begin the cycle again if needed.	*Three of the students are doing well. One still needs my coaching but not direct intervention. Should I go through the routine and change the rewards again?* *Should I check that these students are doing well in the less-structured parts of the day?*	*11/9*

I would like four of my students to begin the instructional day smoothly, forming good habits and contributing to the group instructional time.

Is there anything in particular that struck you about this case? We would like to highlight two interesting features:

1. Four students with the same EF difficulties might not share the same root problem.

2. Parents often hold part of the answer to your mysteries and will engage in the plan if you present it as a plan and not a complaint. We often begin these conversations with "I'm not calling about a problem, more of an opportunity." Parents usually breathe a sigh of relief that is palpable even over the phone lines, and we get to share a quick laugh. Then we begin to plan.

Case 2—Fifteen-Year-Old Girl and Homework

The text of the Case 2 Defining a Dream Questionnaire follows.

Describe your problem of practice:

At mid-quarter, it seems that Suzie has lots of zeros for missing work and is very evasive about what is going on.

1. Why is this issue of central importance to you, your student, your practice, or your school? What are its essential features?

I am concerned that Suzie's grades are low, but more important, she is *not getting the practice* she needs to *solidify the new concepts* we're covering. She is getting good at avoiding other kinds of work now too. It looks like this pattern began about three weeks ago.

2. What are its greatest areas of impact? What else does it impact?

It looks like it is happening in math more than other subjects, but she is *missing work in three of her classes*.

3. How has it been addressed so far, and why does it need to be addressed differently now?

I have been asking her to try harder to get things in and reminding her to write things down. Last week I took her aside and told her just how important this is for her. She seemed to be taking it seriously at the time, but she is missing work this week again—something needs to *change*!

4. Who may be able to help formulate a new plan?

Her other teachers.

Using your responses to the preceding questions, summarize your problem of practice as a more generative dream. If it helps, highlight the $10 words from each of your four responses and use them in your description.

Suzie will use strategies to help her track and turn in her work in all classes in order to increase practice and build stronger concepts. She may need a check-in system at first, but should be able to be successful independently in all classes, including math class.

Is there anything in particular that struck you about this case? We would like to highlight two interesting features:

1. There are students who seem to manage school expectations well most of the time, but who, in fact, are working

Table 7.2   Case 2 Planning and Reflection Guide

Name or Topic:	Area(s) of Need:	Date
Suzie	*Finishing homework and turning it in*	*3/3*
Assessment What do you already know about your student, class(es), program(s), or school(s)? Use observation notes, BRIEFs, formal and informal assessments.	*Teachers report:* *3:5 missing homework in math* *2:4 missing in English* *1:3 missing in history* *Math teacher is concerned about her messy binder.*	*3/3*
Dream Define the dream you will aim for (use the generative dream you created in the Defining a Dream Questionnaire). Are there other issues that can be addressed by that same dream?	*Suzie will use strategies to help her track and turn in her work in all classes in order to increase practice and build stronger concepts. She may need a check-in system at first, but should be able to be successful independently in all classes, including math class.* *There may be two other students who could use help with this.*	*3/3*
Mysteries What do you still need to know in order to act? Are there any assumptions that need to be challenged? Are there resources you need? Are there people, protocols, or permissions you need to gather?	*Did anything else happen three weeks ago—illness, injuries, or family issues?* *Has the level of instruction changed dramatically in math or any of the other classes?* *Are there multiple long-term projects or a heavier homework load in general?* *What does her organization look like: backpack, locker, desk at home?*	*3/3*

Table 7.2   Case 2 Planning and Reflection Guide (*Continued*)

Name or Topic:	Area(s) of Need:	Date
Actions What actions can you take to eliminate the mysteries and attain your dreams?	*Check the attendance record.* *Contact parent about injuries, family issues, and organization.* *Check with instructors about workload.* *Check organization.*	3/3
	Talk with Suzie about why she thinks this is happening now. Agree to a plan once these steps have been taken.	3/8
	Suzie was out with strep throat 3 weeks ago and was lethargic even when she came back. Mom reports that she couldn't keep up on her organization or go for extra help because she was so tired. Mom reports that Suzie usually manages these things with a little help, but after an illness, she seems to lose track and then things just get worse.	
	• *Math teacher will help her organize and will plan a help session or two.* • *Support services will meet about other classes and make a plan if needed.* • *Mom will monitor at home.*	3/15
	Suzie is catching up, but will need weekly organization checks.	
Evidence What specific evidence will indicate that you have closed the gap or reached your goal? Make your "evidence" as specific and observable as possible.	*Suzie will use some kind of planner to track her work.* *She will be able to accurately report how her homework is going.* *She will partner with one other student who is having similar challenges.*	3/3
Pose a question to reassess more broadly and begin the cycle again if needed.	*Is she having any other problems with school at this point?* *Are there others who might benefit from a similar plan?*	3/15

much harder to succeed than we know. An illness or a death in the family can take away just enough time, attention, or energy to overwhelm that student's EF capacity. In a case like this, our most intensive interventions may be short term, but a loose framework of support may be necessary to ensure long-term success.

2. At times a student will have more trouble with organization and executive functioning in one class than another. This can be due to subject-specific organizational demands, teacher styles, or learning style. In any case, as just noted, the combination of demands in that specific class may put one student over the edge in terms of executive functioning, but may show up mildly or not at all in others.

Case 3—Reading as an EF Issue Throughout the School

The text of the Case 3 Defining a Dream Questionnaire follows.

Describe your problem of practice:

A student in *grade 3* is having a lot of trouble with *reading chapter books*. Every time there is a discussion or *comprehension* check on a few chapters, she has a lot of trouble remembering what happened. Her teacher thinks she isn't reading, but her mom insists that she is. She is referred to the reading specialist, who indicates that a *fifth-grade* boy struggles with that same issue. The reading specialist administered an Individual Reading Inventory (IRI) to each, but they each seem to be well in range of the reading comprehension levels needed for their books. Further evaluation indicates that these students have *EF problems and low fluency*. An intervention is needed to help students both increase fluency and understand the text structure embedded in novels and textbooks.

1. Why is this issue of central importance to you, your student, your practice, or your school? What are its essential features?

   The students, teachers, and parents in these cases don't seem to know how to improve comprehension, and it's something that comes up year after year. The problem seems to include lack of reading experience in these students, low fluency, and lack of strategies for identifying and remembering key features.

2. What are its greatest areas of impact? What else does it impact?

   This clearly impacts reading class, but on closer examination, it seems to impact science and history for the older students.

3. How has it been addressed so far, and why does it need to be addressed differently now?

   We have monitored these students to be sure that they are reading. We have previewed vocabulary and big ideas before beginning chapters, and we review together in class. No matter what we do, it's as if these students aren't reading the book at all.

4. Who may be able to help formulate a new plan?
   The classroom teachers, the reading specialist, and the learning specialist.

   Using your responses to the preceding questions, summarize your problem of practice as a more generative dream. If it helps, highlight the $10 words from each of your four responses and use them in your description.
   We will design a school response to address students like these at all levels. We will designate a time in the school day when this can be addressed. We will design a space where brief fluency drills and guided reading can happen without distraction.

Table 7.3   Case 3 Planning and Reflection Guide

Name or Topic:	Area(s) of Need:	Date
Reading comprehension at Jones School	*Instruction aimed at text structure and organization; practice for fluency.*	*2/10*
Assessment What do you already know about your student, class(es), program(s), or school(s)? Use observation notes, BRIEFs, formal and informal assessments.	*These students have solid comprehension scores on the extended reading passages of an IRI.* *These students each have slightly low fluency scores.* *They each have trouble with comprehension checks in class.* *They each have trouble with organizing and prioritizing, according to teacher observations and checklists.* *These students do much better on single chapter reviews or reading using guiding questions.* *Their teachers do a really good job previewing both concepts and vocabulary before they begin a new chapter.*	*2/10*
Dream Define the dream you will aim for (use the generative dream you created in the Defining a Dream Questionnaire). Are there other issues that can be addressed by that same dream?	*We will design a school response to address students like these at all levels. We will designate a time in the school day when this can be addressed. We will design a space where brief fluency drills and guided reading can happen without distraction.*	*2/15*
Mysteries		
What do you still need to know in order to act? Are there any assumptions that need to be challenged? Are there resources you need? Are there people, protocols, or permissions you need to gather?	*We don't know what space could be used.* *We don't know how many other students could use this approach.* *Should we see if there are students with a large number of incompletes in reading assignments who could be struggling with these same issues?* *Are there students with low "effort" grades who could be similarly suffering?*	*2/15*

Table 7.3   Case 3 Planning and Reflection Guide (*Continued*)

Name or Topic:	Area(s) of Need:	Date
	Are there volunteers who could help with the fluency drills at the beginning of the day?	
	Would this interfere with any other initiative in the school right now? Would it complement one?	
Actions What actions can you take to eliminate the mysteries and attain your dreams?	*At the next faculty meeting, we will ask teachers to identify students who have a large number of incompletes or low effort in reading assignments.*	*2/15*
	We will check with administration to see if there is a small quiet space that could be used once or twice during the day for this purpose. Also check to see what other initiatives are being planned right now.	
	Once we identify the number of students who need this, we will need to determine groupings and times of day for practice.	*2/22*
	We have found 5 students who may fit this profile. Our reading specialist still needs to test 2 of them to be certain.	
	We have a small room in the library that is not being used at the beginning of the day, after lunch, or at the end of the day. We could schedule it for 15 minutes each time if needed.	
	New initiative: The new reading curriculum stresses text-marking but not fluency. We will need to be certain that teachers emphasize text-marking, which means we won't need instructional time for this in our small sessions, just practice time. Fluency is not emphasized strongly enough for these students.	
	Consider: 15-minute sessions with the reading specialist for "warm-ups" every morning in the library, 3 students at a time. They can use old magazines (written at their reading level) from our library to read for pleasure and guided text-marking, while our reading specialist meets with one at a time to spend three minutes on Great Leaps with each. Once this routine is going well, perhaps we can use a parent volunteer or assistant to continue this while our reading specialist begins another group in another room.	

(*Continued*)

Table 7.3   Case 3 Planning and Reflection Guide (*Continued*)

Name or Topic:	Area(s) of Need:	Date
	Question: *Will magazines be enough, or will we need to use copies of their actual novels?*	
	It seems we have 5 students who need this, so we will proceed with the above plan, rechecking their reading levels and classroom progress in early April.	2/28
Evidence What specific evidence will indicate that you have closed the gap or reached your goal? Make your "evidence" as specific and observable as possible.	*We expect to see increased fluency, text-marking, and discussion in the small-group sessions.* *We expect to see improved comprehension and reading performance in the classroom.*	2/15
Pose a question to reassess more broadly and begin the cycle again if needed.	*Can the improved levels be sustained without continued practice? How will we know?*	2/15

Is there anything in particular that struck you about this case? We would like to highlight a few interesting features:

1. Some reading comprehension problems stem from problems with decoding, background knowledge, vocabulary, lack of experience, or higher-level thinking abilities. But when these features are intact, consider the possibility of EF difficulties in terms of the student's ability to organize and prioritize *as he or she layers increasingly complex levels of information on top of each other.*

2. Although reading fluency is not solely an issue of executive functioning, an increased level of automaticity in any

subject improves the effectiveness and efficiency of working memory—a key feature of the executive skills.

3. Lack of experience or practice in reading can lead to problems of fluency and the ability to anticipate text structure. Practicing executive skills while reading topics of a student's own choice addresses multiple issues, and anchors the practice in a genre the student is most likely to use.

PLAN TO MONITOR

Although we'd all like to think that once we solve a problem it stays solved, we also know that that's just not true. You need to count on cycles of action and reflection because your students change, the curriculum changes, the seasons change, and you change. However, if you have invested some time and energy in creating an EF-Smart Classroom and you make use of the specialists in your school to help you plan for EF-smart individuals, the ebb and flow of your challenges can be minimized.

Our final piece of advice—**use a calendar**. When you make a plan for change, be sure to mark the days you will return to assess your plan. Be certain to give your students time to change, because creating new habits takes at least three weeks—and more to become independent, for most students.

Finally, perhaps we all should take a highlighter to our calendars and mark off the most stressful times of the school year.

1. The first six weeks of the school year and returning from breaks (transitions, new routines)

2. Before holidays (increased stress, disrupted routines)

3. The end of each quarter (increased work, increased stress over grades for some)

4. The beginning of a new quarter (low energy resulting from high stress at the end of the previous quarter)

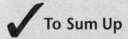

To Sum Up

- Classroom and school changes in routines can improve the executive skills of all students and teachers. We can plan for gentle change that minimizes stress by using a simple planning guide.

- Just as each classroom and school is unique, our plans for change should respect those distinctions.

- Your plans to improve the EF skills of students in your school may target individuals, small groups, or the whole school, depending on your most pressing problem(s) of practice.

- Teamwork often works best for defining a school's EF needs and for creating plans to change.

- Sustained cycles of action and reflection will be required in order to create and maintain solid change over time.

- Strong executive skills are so essential to learning and performance that devoting time to addressing these in a mindful way can dramatically change the outcomes for students, classes, and schools.

? Time to Reflect

You've been answering questions throughout the chapter, so we haven't added more here. Please note any other key takeaways:

_____

_____

_____

Conclusion: Helping All Students Blossom

In drawing this book to a close, we decided to borrow from a strategy that is used by creative writers. We take two big steps back and pose an important question: This is a book about executive functioning, but what is it *really* about? For us the answer is easy: gardening.

From a distance, a garden is an impressionistic field of color and shape. Up close, each plant reveals itself. A dedicated gardener appreciates the unique beauty of each plant and understands its specific characteristics and needs.

Some plants fit easily into the landscape—they are natives to the environment and thrive on the exact conditions offered. Others require more pampering to grow well.

Whereas some plants burst from the ground with the first promise of spring, others take more time and require patience. Until their flowers bloom, these slower growers may challenge the gardener to find something appealing about the color or shape of its leaves.

In other parts of the garden, the gardener we must routinely prop up a weak-stemmed plant or build a trellis to allow plants like the vining rose to climb. She knows that these supports will provide the best opportunity for these particular plants to develop to their full glory.

Experienced gardeners also know that some plants grow spindly because their needs are overshadowed by more robust plants. Their energy gets diverted into growing tall enough to grab some sunlight, and in doing so they may become less sturdy. These are the plants the gardener may dig out and move. In another part of the garden, they are able to get their full share of sunlight and grow into strong, beautiful specimens.

Each garden is different—each plant unique. And each gardener must develop his or her own important insights and routines in order to bring each plant into full bloom.

———————————

We wish you the best as you move forward in your very important work of cultivating success in your students and in your schools. We hope we have been able to assist you in some ways by providing glimpses into the thoughts and work of others in the field. We hope to meet some of you in the future and find new ways to share our commitment to education.

Appendix A: The Top Three Accommodations for Students with EF Problems

W hile students with EF weaknesses have unique learning styles with varying levels of impact, there are three accommodations that are frequently recommended following formal evaluation. We believe these important accommodations deserve a brief explanation and some suggestions for how to implement them in a busy classroom.

EXTRA TIME AND/OR REDUCED ASSIGNMENTS AS NEEDED

This is probably one of the most common accommodations made for students with EF problems regardless of the primary cause (for example, attention or anxiety). This accommodation works not only because it allows extra processing time, but also because it reduces stress.

Let's consider two questions that are rarely explicitly addressed in an intervention plan:

When should a teacher provide extra time rather than reducing an assignment?

Should a student receive extra time on an assignment after missing a deadline?

These are great questions posed by sensitive teachers in the field, and fortunately the answers are fairly straightforward.

Think of extra time and reduced assignments as points on a continuum. First, allow extra time on tests and assignments as needed in order to allow students to demonstrate their understanding. However, if that extra time becomes so extensive that it begins to deplete the student, or cuts into other important parts of the student's day, consider reducing the assignment itself until a balance between the assignment and the student's ability is achieved. As long as the essential elements of a unit or assignment are not eliminated, the modified assessment should still be a valid measure of student understanding.

We believe that 100 percent extra time is too much for most students unless they have a severely reduced class load that allows them to make good use of the extra time. Even then, the value of such a lengthy assessment should be weighed carefully against the depleting effect of so much time spent on a single task.

Next, should a student receive extra time on an assignment after missing a deadline? While we believe a student with EF weakness may miss deadlines from time to time, we also believe it is poor practice to allow this to happen repeatedly.

We like to view a missed deadline as a sign of a missing strategy or habit and use that opportunity to re-explore that student's skills. A missed deadline is not a good example of "extra time as needed"—a proactive extension of time is a much more appropriate accommodation.

COPY OF TEACHER NOTES

With updated educational research and good teaching practices, the problem of note taking is becoming less and less of an issue for many teachers and students. At one time it was thought that it was a student's job to take copious notes that were neat and well organized, all while internalizing the main ideas of a lecture. While this may be an admirable skill in some situations, we find that more and more teachers are beginning to offer handouts or electronic templates that highlight the major concepts using titles and subtitles as guides. Or, they may simply provide handouts that outline a new topic and use class time to engage in class discussion of that topic.

That said, there are still times when note taking is an important skill to develop in the classroom. And wouldn't "giving copies of notes" deprive the student of the opportunity to develop that skill? Possibly.

If the student's evaluation results and teacher observations confirm that the student is capable of note taking, then we like to ask students to take their own notes in class even though they will receive a copy of teacher notes afterwards. After class, they can compare their own notes to the teacher's model and see where they might improve. Over time, this activity becomes a form of guided instruction that helps students develop their own organization of ideas while taking notes.

We do like to emphasize, however, that while guided note taking *may* enhance organization of thought, this is not always true. Some students have so much trouble with working memory that listening, organizing, and taking notes all at the same time may just be too much and cause them to misunderstand the important points of a lecture.

How can a teacher tell when this is happening? By checking for understanding orally during instruction.

If a student cannot demonstrate their understanding orally in class, there is a chance that the task of note taking may be interfering. The student should simply be given a copy of the notes so they can engage through listening and asking questions instead.

TESTING IN A SEPARATE ENVIRONMENT AS NEEDED

Testing in a separate environment is a fairly simple accommodation that allows the student freedom from distractions and from the anxiety of wondering "is somebody already on page two before me?" or "Is everybody ahead of me?" However, there are two sides to this accommodation that should be discussed with each student.

When a student takes a test in a separate environment, someone other than the student's teacher proctors the test in most cases. Both teachers and students tell us that this is not always helpful, since the proctor may not be able to address content-based clarifying questions during the test as effectively as the teacher. So, unless we are *certain* that a student's distractibility and anxiety are so significant that they outweigh these other concerns, we like to give students a choice on this accommodation.

_____

What these three important accommodations for students with EF problems have in common is that they help students optimize learning and performance with an emphasis on building and demonstrating their true understanding of concepts.

In the end, it is not always important to simply complete every activity in a timely fashion or engage in a particular measure of assessment. Rather, it is more essential that each student build a personal and complex understanding of the world and demonstrate their understanding in a unique and competent way. These accommodations, when applied sensitively, help students accomplish this in spite of their EF challenges.

Appendix B: Accessing the Online Materials

You can access free downloadable versions of a number of the tools found in this book on the Jossey-Bass website. Just go to www.josseybass.com/go/executive function, and you can download a zip file containing the following materials:

Figure 3.1: Tools and Targets for Self-Evaluation

Table 4.1: Specific Interventions for Specific Targets

Figure 7.1: Defining a Dream Questionnaire

Figure 7.2: Planning and Reflection Guide

Blank versions of the following are also included:

Figure 4.1: Student Planner

Figure 4.3: Graphic Organizer created with Inspiration Software

Please feel free to use each tool as-is or customize it for your own classroom. We hope you find these materials useful.

Endnotes

CHAPTER 1

1. Suchy, Y. "Executive Functioning: Overview, Assessment, and Research Issues for Non-Neuropsychologists." *Annals of Behavioral Medicine*, 2009, 37(2), 106–116.
2. Gioia, G. A., Isquith, P. K., Guy, S. C., and Kenworthy, L. *Behavior Rating Inventory of Executive Function, Professional Manual.* Odessa, FL: Psychological Assessment Resources, 2000.
3. Gioia, G. A., Isquith, P. K., Retzlaff, P. D., and Espy, K. A. "Confirmatory Factor Analysis of the Behavior Rating Inventory of Executive Function (BRIEF) in a Clinical Sample." *Clinical Neuropsychology*, 2002, 8(4), 249–257.

CHAPTER 2

1. Barkley, R. A. *ADHD and the Nature of Self-Control.* New York: Guilford Press, 1997; Brown, T. E. "Emerging Understandings of Attention Deficit Disorders and Comorbidities." In T. E. Brown (ed.), *Attention Deficit Disorders and Comorbidities in Children, Adolescents and Adults* (pp. 3–55). Washington, DC: American Psychiatric Press, 2000.
2. For a review, see Brown, R. T., and others. "Treatment of Attention-Deficit/Hyperactivity Disorder: Overview of the Evidence." *Pediatrics*, 2005, 115(6), 749–757. http://pediatrics.aappublications.org/content/115/6/e749.
3. Robinson, S., and others. "Executive Functions in Children with Autism Spectrum Disorders." *Brain and Cognition*, 2009, 71(3), 362–368.

4. Kaplan, S., and Berman, M. G. "Directed Attention as a Common Resource for Executive Functioning and Self-Regulation." *Perspectives on Psychological Science,* 2010, *5*(1), 43–57.

5. Arnsten, A. "The Biology of Being Frazzled." *Science,* 1998, *280*(5370), 1711–1712.

6. Selye, H. *The Stress of Life.* New York: McGraw-Hill, 1956.

7. For a review, see Center on the Developing Child at Harvard University. *Building the Brain's "Air Traffic Control" System: How Early Experiences Shape the Development of Executive Function: Working Paper No. 11.* Cambridge, MA: Center on the Developing Child at Harvard University, 2011. http://developingchild.harvard.edu/index.php/download_file/-/view/836/.

8. Ibid.

9. Micco, J. A., and others. "Executive Functioning in Offspring at Risk for Depression and Anxiety." *Depression and Anxiety,* 2009, *26*(9), 780–790.

10. Kaplan and Berman, "Directed Attention"; Ratey, J. *Spark.* New York: Little, Brown, 2008.

11. Kaplan and Berman, "Directed Attention."

12. Cooper-Kahn, J., and Dietzel, L. *Late, Lost and Unprepared: A Parent's Guide to Helping Children with Executive Functioning.* Bethesda, MD: Woodbine House, 2008.

13. Powell, K. B. and Voeller, K.K.S. "Prefrontal Executive Function Syndromes in Children." *Journal of Child Neurology,* 2004, *19*(10), 785–797.

CHAPTER 3

1. Dehn, M. J. *Working Memory and Academic Learning: Assessment and Intervention.* Hoboken, NJ: Wiley, 2008, p. 286.

2. Washburn, K. "Guest Blog: Report from the Learning and Brain Conference." http://www.edutopia.org/kevin-washburn-learning-brain-intelligence-factors. Mar. 2010.

3. Senge, P. "Creating Quality Communities." http://www.solonline.org/res/kr/qualcom.html. 1999. This site is no longer available.

CHAPTER 4

1. Gioia, G. A., Isquith, P. K., Guy, S. C., and Kenworthy, L. *Behavior Rating Inventory of Executive Function, Professional Manual.* Odessa, FL: Psychological Assessment Resources, 2000.

CHAPTER 5

1. Hale, J. B. "Response to Intervention: Guidelines for Parents and Practitioners." http://www.wrightslaw.com/idea/art/rti .hale.htm. Mar. 2008.
2. McDonald, J. P., Mohr, N., Dichter, A., and McDonald, E. C. *The Power of Protocols: an Educator's Guide to Better Practice.* New York: Teachers College Press, 2003.

CHAPTER 6

1. Anderson, L. W., and Krathwohl, D. R. (eds.). *A Taxonomy for Learning, Teaching, and Assessing: A Revision of Bloom's Taxonomy of Educational Objectives.* New York: Longman, 2001, p. 268.
2. Greber, C., Ziviani, J., and Rodger, S. "The Four-Quadrant Model of Facilitated Learning (Part 2): Strategies and Applications." *Australian Occupational Therapy Journal,* 2007, 54(Suppl. 1), S40–S48.
3. Ibid., p. S40.
4. Ibid., p. S42.
5. Ibid., p. S43.
6. Ibid., p. S45.

CHAPTER 7

1. Lavoie, R. *How Difficult Can This Be? The F.A.T. City Workshop.* Alexandria, VA: PBS, 1989. Video.

Index